UNLOCK

READING & WRITING SKILLS

4

Chris Sowton

CAMBRIDGE
UNIVERSITY PRESS

CAMBRIDGE
UNIVERSITY PRESS

University Printing House, Cambridge CB2 8BS, United Kingdom

Cambridge University Press is part of the University of Cambridge.

It furthers the University's mission by disseminating knowledge in the pursuit of education, learning and research at the highest international levels of excellence.

www.cambridge.org
Information on this title: www.cambridge.org/9781107615250

First published 2014

Printed in China by Golden Cup Printing Co. Ltd

A catalogue record for this publication is available from the British Library

ISBN 978-1-107-61525-0 Reading and Writing 4 Student's Book with Online Workbook
ISBN 978-1-107-61409-3 Reading and Writing 4 Teacher's Book with DVD
ISBN 978-1-107-63461-9 Listening and Speaking 4 Student's Book with Online Workbook
ISBN 978-1-107-65052-7 Listening and Speaking 4 Teacher's Book with DVD

Additional resources for this publication at www.cambridge.org/unlock

BN

CONTENTS

MAP OF THE BOOK

UNIT	VIDEO	READING	VOCABULARY		
1 GLOBALIZATION Reading 1: Turkish treats (Media) Reading 2: What impact has globalization had on food and eating habits in Italy? (Economics)	A world of food in one city	**Key reading skill**: Making predictions from a text type Using your knowledge to predict content Understanding key vocabulary Making inferences from the text Reading for main ideas Identifying purpose and audience	Academic alternatives to phrasal verbs (e.g. *increase, continue, study*) Globalization vocabulary (e.g. *consumption, obesity, multinational*)		
2 EDUCATION Reading 1: Preparing for success, whatever you want to do (Higher education) Reading 2: Distance or face-to-face learning – what's the difference? (Electronic learning)	Becoming a gondolier	**Key reading skill**: Making inferences from the text Understanding key vocabulary Vocabulary in context Reading for detail Reading for main ideas	Education vocabulary (e.g. *assignment, examination, dissertation*) Academic words (e.g. *establishment, motivation, interaction*)		
3 MEDICINE Reading 1: The homeopathy debate (Medical ethics) Reading 2: Should healthcare be free? (Economics)	Alternative medicine	**Key reading skill**: Skimming for key words Reading for detail Identifying opinions Understanding key vocabulary Scanning to find key words Making inferences from the text	Medical vocabulary (e.g. *cosmetic surgery, preventable illness, disease epidemic*) Academic vocabulary (e.g. *complex, illegal, adequate*)		
4 RISK Reading 1: Are you a risk-taker, or are you risk-adverse? (Psychology) Reading 2: A government has a duty to protect its citizens from personal, professional and financial risk (Public administration)	Roller coasters	**Key reading skill**: Previewing a topic before reading Understanding key vocabulary Reading for main ideas Reading for detail Using your knowledge to predict content Scanning to find information Making inferences from the text	Language of freedom (e.g. *allow, ban, limit*) Academic nouns (e.g. *regulations, legislation, prevention*)		
5 MANUFACTURING Reading 1: A brief history of silk (History) Reading 2: How is paper manufactured? (Manufacturing systems)	Making chocolate	**Key reading skill**: Activating prior knowledge Reading for detail Making inferences from the text Using your knowledge to predict content Reading for main ideas Reading for detail Making inferences from the text	Academic verb synonyms (e.g. *alter, distribute, extract*) Nominalization		

GRAMMAR	CRITICAL THINKING	WRITING
Grammar for writing: • Noun phrases • Time phrases	• Understand providing supporting examples • Apply supporting examples to statements	*Academic writing skills*: • Essay types • Essay structure *Writing task type*: Write the first draft of an essay. *Writing task*: How have food and eating habits changed in your country? Suggest some reasons for these changes.
Grammar for writing: • Comparison and contrast language • Comparison and contrast language in topic sentences	• Analyze academic and vocational subjects	*Academic writing skills*: Analyzing an essay question *Writing task type*: Write an introduction to an essay (1). *Writing task*: Outline the various differences between studying a language and studying mathematics. In what ways may they in fact be similar?
Grammar for writing: • Articles • Language of concession	• Evaluate actions for avoiding illness • Understand whether statements are in favour or against an argument	*Academic writing skills*: Write an introduction to an essay (2) *Writing task type*: Structure body paragraphs in an essay. *Writing task*: 'Avoiding preventable illnesses is the responsibility of individuals and their families, not governments.' Do you agree?
Grammar for writing: • Cause and effect • Conditional language	• Evaluate risks • Apply risk evaluation	*Academic writing skills*: Topic sentences in body paragraphs *Writing task type*: Structure 'for and against' arguments in essays. *Writing task*: 'If children are never exposed to risk, they will never be able to cope with risk.' Give reasons for and against this statement and give your opinion.
Grammar for writing: • The passive • Sequencing	• Understand the stages in a process • Apply understanding of the stages in a process	*Academic writing skills*: Adding detail to your writing *Writing task type:* Write a description of a process. *Writing task*: Write a description of a process with which you are familiar.

UNIT	VIDEO	READING	VOCABULARY	
6 ENVIRONMENT Reading 1: Disaster mitigation (Meteorology) Reading 2: Combating drought in rural Africa: a report (Environment)	The Three Gorges Dam	*Key reading skill*: Identify cohesive devices (pronouns and synonyms) Understanding key vocabulary Reading for main ideas Reading for detail Making inferences from the text Using your knowledge to predict content	Natural disaster vocabulary (e.g. *natural, major, severe*) Academic noun phrases	
7 ARCHITECTURE Reading 1: Are green buildings too costly? (Environmental planning) Reading 2: Which is more important when designing a building: beauty or function? (Building design)	Islamic architecture	*Key reading skill*: Skimming Using your knowledge to predict content Understanding key vocabulary Reading for detail Making inferences from the text Reading for main ideas	Academic word families (e.g. *function, environment, responsibility*) Architecture and planning (e.g. *conservation, skyscrapers, outskirts*)	
8 ENERGY Reading 1: Slides from a presentation on energy (Energy development) Reading 2: The world is running out of many vital natural resources. Discuss the most effective ways to address this problem. (Environment)	Alternative energy	*Key reading skill*: Working out meaning from context Understanding key vocabulary Reading for detail Using your knowledge to predict content Making inferences from the text	Energy collocations (e.g. *fossil fuel, renewable energy, air pollution*) Formal and informal academic verbs (e.g. *consult, deliver, instigate*)	
9 ART Reading 1: Art for art's sake? (Fine art) Reading 2: Should photography be considered a fine art, like painting or sculpture? (Photography)	Art and design (A Leonardo da Vinci design)	*Key reading skill*: Scanning to find information Understanding key vocabulary Using your knowledge to predict content Reading for detail Making inferences from the text Paraphrasing	Quotations and reporting information (e.g. *state, say, argue*) Describing art (e.g. *abstract, figurative, lifelike*)	
10 AGEING Reading 1: The social and economic impact of ageing (Economics) Reading 2: What are the effects of a young population on a society? (Social anthropology)	The Khanty of Siberia	*Key reading skill*: Using your knowledge to predict content Reading for detail Making inferences from the text Understanding key vocabulary Reading for main ideas Working out meaning from context	Retirement and the elderly (e.g. *pension, retirement, memory*) Academic collocations with prepositions (e.g. *rely on, in contrast, range of*)	

GRAMMAR	CRITICAL THINKING	WRITING
Grammar for writing: • Expressing solutions using *it*	• Analyze strategies • Create a diagram analyzing strategies in terms of cost and time	*Academic writing skills*: Paragraph structure in essays *Writing task type:* Write a report referring to a case study. *Writing task*: Write a report which provides both short- and long-term solutions to an environmental problem. Refer to a specific case study in your report.
Grammar for writing: • Register in academic writing	• Evaluate arguments • Analyze arguments	*Academic writing skills*: Ordering information *Writing task type:* Write a persuasive essay *Writing task*: Which is more important when building or buying a new home: its location or its size?
Grammar for writing: • Relative clauses • Defining and non-defining relative clauses • Phrases to introduce advantages and disadvantages	• Evaluate your answers to a questionnaire • Understand alternative energy sources	*Academic writing skills*: Editing language Spelling Countable/uncountable nouns *Writing task type:* Write a problem–solution essay. *Writing task*: The world is unable to meet its energy needs. What three sources of renewable energy would be most effective in solving this problem in your country? Which is your preferred option?
Grammar for writing: • Substitution • Ellipsis	• Understand supporting and challenging statements • Evaluate statements	*Academic writing skills*: Coherence *Writing task type:* Write an essay using quotations. *Writing task*: Fashion, cooking, video games and sport have all been likened to fine art. Choose *one* of these and discuss whether it should be considered fine art, comparable to painting or sculpture.
Grammar for writing: • Numerical words and phrases • Language of prediction	• Analyze data • Apply data analysis • Understand advantages	*Academic writing skills*: Interpreting graphs and charts *Writing task type:* Describe population data and its implications. *Writing task*: The population pyramids show the global population by age in 1950 and 2010 and the projected figures for 2100. Write an essay describing the information and suggesting what the potential global impact could be if the 2100 projections are correct.

UNL⌀CK UNIT STRUCTURE

The units in *Unlock Reading & Writing Skills* are carefully scaffolded so that students are taken step-by-step through the writing process.

UNLOCK YOUR KNOWLEDGE | Encourages discussion around the theme of the unit with inspiration from interesting questions and striking visuals.

WATCH AND LISTEN | Features an engaging and motivating *Discovery Education*™ video which generates interest in the topic.

READING 1 | Practises the reading skills required to understand academic texts as well as the vocabulary needed to comprehend the text itself.

READING 2 | Presents a second text which provides a different angle on the topic in a different genre. It is a model text for the writing task.

LANGUAGE DEVELOPMENT | Practises the vocabulary and grammar from the Readings in preparation for the writing task.

CRITICAL THINKING | Contains brainstorming, evaluative and analytical tasks as preparation for the writing task.

GRAMMAR FOR WRITING | Presents and practises grammatical structures and features needed for the writing task.

ACADEMIC WRITING SKILLS | Practises all the writing skills needed for the writing task.

WRITING TASK | Uses the skills and language learnt over the course of the unit to draft and edit the writing task. Requires students to produce a piece of academic writing. Checklists help learners to edit their work.

OBJECTIVES REVIEW | Allows students to assess how well they have mastered the skills covered in the unit.

WORDLIST | Includes the key vocabulary from the unit.

This is the unit's main learning objective. It gives learners the opportunity to use all the language and skills they have learnt in the unit.

UNLCK MOTIVATION

UNL◯CK YOUR KNOWLEDGE ● ● ● ● ● ● ● ● ● ● ● ●

Work with a partner. Discuss the questions below.

1 Look at your clothes, the items on your desk, in your bag and pockets. Where were they made? How many were made in your country?
2 Does it matter that we now import so many goods from other countries? Why? / Why not?
3 What effects has globalization had on your country?

PERSONALIZE

Unlock encourages students to bring their own knowledge, experiences and opinions to the topics. This motivates students to relate the topics to their own contexts.

DISCOVERY EDUCATION™ VIDEO

Thought-provoking videos from *Discovery Education™* are included in every unit throughout the course to introduce topics, promote discussion and motivate learners. The videos provide a new angle on a wide range of academic subjects.

"
The video was excellent! It helped with raising students' interest in the topic. It was well-structured and the language level was appropriate.

Maria Agata Szczerbik,
United Arab Emirates University,
Al-Ain, UAE
"

UNL⌀CK CRITICAL THINKING

> " The Critical thinking sections present a difficult area in an engaging and accessible way.
>
> Shirley Norton, London School of English, UK "

BLOOM'S TAXONOMY

CREATE — create, invent, plan, compose, construct, design, imagine

decide, rate, choose, recommend, justify, assess, prioritize — **EVALUATE**

ANALYZE — explain, contrast, examine, identify, investigate, categorize

show, complete, use, classify, examine, illustrate, solve — **APPLY**

UNDERSTAND — compare, discuss, restate, predict, translate, outline

name, describe, relate, find, list, write, tell — **REMEMBER**

BLOOM'S TAXONOMY

The Critical Thinking sections in *Unlock* are based on Benjamin Bloom's classification of learning objectives. This ensures learners develop their **lower-** and **higher-order thinking skills**, ranging from demonstrating **knowledge** and **understanding** to in-depth **evaluation**.

The margin headings in the Critical Thinking sections highlight the exercises which develop Bloom's concepts.

LEARN TO THINK

Learners engage in **evaluative** and **analytical tasks** that are designed to ensure they do all of the thinking and information-gathering required for the end-of-unit writing task.

CRITICAL THINKING

At the end of this unit, you will write the first draft of an essay. Look at this unit's writing task in the box below.

> How have food and eating habits changed in your country? Suggest some reasons for the changes.

UNDERSTAND

Providing supporting examples

In academic writing, you need to justify and give supporting examples to any statements or opinions that you write, to show that they are true.

UNLOCK RESEARCH

THE CAMBRIDGE LEARNER CORPUS ◉

The **Cambridge Learner Corpus** is a bank of official Cambridge English exam papers. Our exclusive access means we can use the corpus to carry out unique research and identify the most common errors learners make. That information is used to ensure the *Unlock* syllabus teaches the most **relevant language**.

THE WORDS YOU NEED

Language Development sections provide vocabulary and grammar building tasks that are further practised in the **UNL☉CK ONLINE** Workbook.
The glossary and end-of-unit wordlists provide definitions, pronunciation and handy summaries of all the key vocabulary.

GLOBALIZATION   UNIT 1

◉ LANGUAGE DEVELOPMENT

EXPLANATION

Academic alternatives to phrasal verbs

When writing essays, it is important to use language which is more formal than you would use when speaking or in informal pieces of writing.

Phrasal verbs, which usually consist of a main verb followed by a particle (e.g. *up*, *on*), are less common in academic writing than in informal writing. In academic writing, phrasal verbs can often be replaced by a single word. Using these alternatives will make your writing seem more formal and academic.

GRAMMAR FOR WRITING

EXPLANATION

Noun phrases

Nouns are often combined with other words to make noun phrases. These can express a more specific idea.

Noun phrases can be made by combining nouns with:

- other nouns: *building regulations*
- relative clauses: *a building which is very old*
- prepositional phrases: *the building at the back*
- adjectives: *the tall, white building*

ACADEMIC LANGUAGE

Unique research using the **Cambridge English Corpus** has been carried out into academic language, in order to provide learners with relevant, academic vocabulary from the start (CEFR A1 and above). This addresses a gap in current academic vocabulary mapping and ensures learners are presented with carefully selected words they will find essential during their studies.

GRAMMAR FOR WRITING

The grammar syllabus is carefully designed to help learners become good writers of English. There is a strong focus on sentence structure, word agreement and referencing, which are important for **coherent** and **organized** academic writing.

> The language development is clear and the strong lexical focus is positive as learners feel they make more progress when they learn more vocabulary.

Colleen Wackrow,
Princess Nourah Bint Abdulrahman University, Al-Riyadh, Kingdom of Saudi Arabia

UNLOCK SOLUTIONS

FLEXIBLE

Unlock is available in a range of print and digital components, so teachers can mix and match according to their requirements.

UNLOCK ONLINE WORKBOOKS

The **UNLOCK ONLINE** Workbooks are accessed via activation codes packaged with the Student's Books. These **easy-to-use** workbooks provide interactive exercises, games, tasks, and further practice of the language and skills from the Student's Books in the Cambridge LMS, an engaging and modern learning environment.

CAMBRIDGE LEARNING MANAGEMENT SYSTEM (LMS)

The Cambridge LMS provides teachers with the ability to track learner progress and save valuable time thanks to automated marking functionality. Blogs, forums and other tools are also available to facilitate communication between students and teachers.

UNLOCK EBOOKS

The *Unlock* Student's Books and Teacher's Books are also available as interactive eBooks. With answers and *Discovery Education*™ videos embedded, the eBooks provide a great alternative to the printed materials.

COURSE COMPONENTS

- Each level of *Unlock* consists of two Student's Books: **Reading & Writing** and **Listening & Speaking** and an accompanying Teacher's Book for each. Online Workbooks are packaged with each Student's Book.
- Look out for the symbols in the Student's Books which indicate that additional practice of that skill or language area is available in the Online Workbook.
- Every *Unlock* Student's Book is delivered both in print format and as an interactive **eBook for tablet devices**.
- The *Unlock* Teacher's Books contain additional writing tasks, tests, teaching tips and research projects for students.
- *Presentation Plus* **software for interactive whiteboards** is available for all Student's Books.

READING AND WRITING

Student's Book and Online Workbook Pack*	978-1-107-61399-7	978-1-107-61400-0	978-1-107-61526-7	978-1-107-61525-0
Teacher's Book with DVD*	978-1-107-61401-7	978-1-107-61403-1	978-1-107-61404-8	978-1-107-61409-3
Presentation Plus (interactive whiteboard software)	978-1-107-63800-6	978-1-107-65605-5	978-1-107-67624-4	978-1-107-68245-0

*eBook available from **www.cambridge.org/unlock**

LISTENING AND SPEAKING

Student's Book and Online Workbook Pack*	978-1-107-67810-1	978-1-107-68232-0	978-1-107-68728-8	978-1-107-63461-9
Teacher's Book with DVD*	978-1-107-66211-7	978-1-107-64280-5	978-1-107-68154-5	978-1-107-65052-7
Presentation Plus (interactive whiteboard software)	978-1-107-66424-1	978-1-107-69582-5	978-1-107-63543-2	978-1-107-64381-9

*eBook available from **www.cambridge.org/unlock**

The complete course audio is available from
www.cambridge.org/unlock

LEARNING OBJECTIVES

Watch and listen	Watch and understand a video about a world of food in one city
Reading skills	Make predictions from text types
Academic writing skills	Recognize essay types and essay structures
Writing task	Write the first draft of an essay

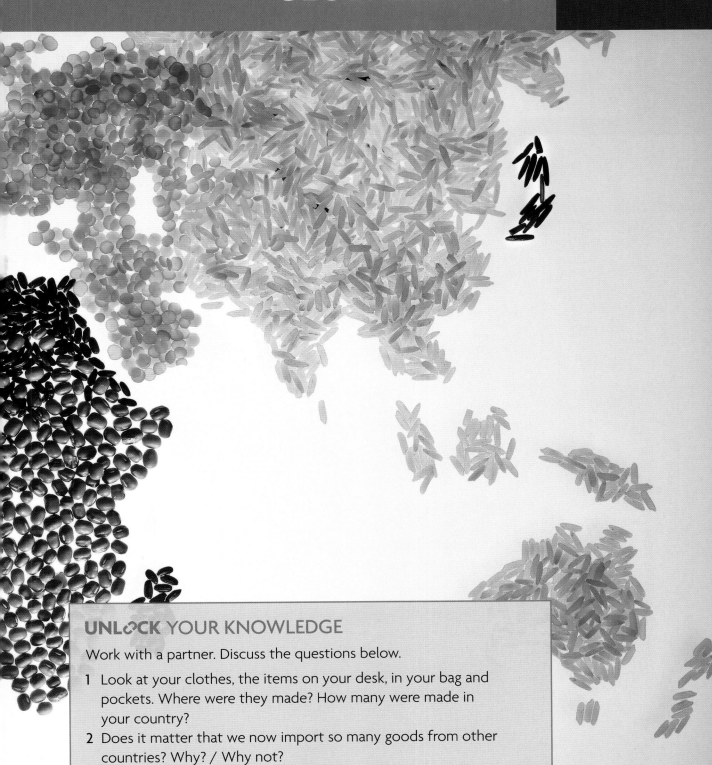

GLOBALIZATION UNIT 1

UNLOCK YOUR KNOWLEDGE

Work with a partner. Discuss the questions below.

1 Look at your clothes, the items on your desk, in your bag and pockets. Where were they made? How many were made in your country?

2 Does it matter that we now import so many goods from other countries? Why? / Why not?

3 What effects has globalization had on your country?

PREPARING TO WATCH

UNDERSTANDING KEY VOCABULARY

1 Complete the sentences below with a word or phrase from the box.

> ethnic groups   South American   cooking equipment
> international media   prepared food   IT communication   labour
> international cuisine

1 Another phrase for 'economic migration' is the flow of
_____ .

2 CNN, the BBC and Al Jazeera are examples of
_____ .

3 Email and social-media sites are the most commonly used forms
of _____ .

4 Italian-Americans and Korean-Americans are two of the largest
_____ which live in New York.

5 Peru, Brazil and Colombia are all _____
countries.

6 Ready-made sauces and frozen soup are types of
_____ .

7 Pots, saucepans and woks are all types of _____ .

8 Curry, dumplings and pizza are all examples of
_____ .

USING YOUR KNOWLEDGE TO PREDICT CONTENT

2 You are going to watch a video about food in New York. Before you
watch, look at the photos and ask and answer the questions with
a partner.

1 What do you know about New York?
2 What types of food is the USA famous for?
3 There are many different types of restaurant in New York. Why do you
think this is?

3 Watch the video. Were your predictions correct?

WHILE WATCHING

4 ▶ Watch again. Complete the notes below with one word in each gap.

New York: from melting pot to cooking pot
- International trade routes, migration, (1)_____ and IT communication expand across (2)_____ borders.
- Different cultures interact more, with a flow of goods, (3)_____ and ideas.
- Globalization is common all over the world but there are certain cities where this is more (4)_____ than others.

New York:
- The best example of a city where different (5)_____ have come together through globalization.
- A centre for (6)_____ for hundreds of years.
- Home to many (7)_____ groups.
- Huge (8)_____ of world food on sale.
- Took immigrant food and changed it to create a new American (9)_____ .

---

5 Work with a partner. Answer the questions below. Work out the meaning from the context.

1 What does *a flow of goods* mean?
  a more imported and exported products
  b an increase of skilful immigrants
  c an increase in migration
  d more trade routes in New York

2 Ethnic communities in New York gave traditional foods *a twist*. What does this mean?
  a They changed the food beyond recognition.
  b They maintained traditional methods.
  c They ignored traditional foods.
  d They created something new based on traditional food.

3 What does *Afro-American* food mean?
  a food from Africa which is exported to the USA
  b a combination of food from South America and Africa
  c pre-prepared rice and chicken dishes in supermarkets
  d food made by the descendents of African migrants

4 Why is New York called *a melting pot*?
  a A huge variety of food is cooked there.
  b There are over 19,000 restaurants.
  c It is home to many ethnic groups.
  d Because it has international trade routes.

DISCUSSION

6 Work with a partner. Discuss the questions below.

1 Why do you think people from so many different countries moved to New York?

2 What influence has US culture had on the food and restaurants of other countries?

3 Which other cultures have had an influence on the food in your country?

READING 1

PREPARING TO READ

Making predictions from a text type

Different text types (such as essays, articles and blogs) have different characteristics. Some will be more suitable for academic study than others. Before reading a text, we can make predictions about the information and the style of the writing. The source, title and any pictures can help us predict the content.

USING YOUR KNOWLEDGE TO PREDICT CONTENT

1 You are going to read part of a blog. Before reading, which of the statements below do you think will be true?

1 The style will be informal.

2 The contents will be appropriate for an academic essay.

3 The writer will give his or her personal opinions.

4 The information will be up-to-date.

2 Read the blog and check your predictions. Find examples to support your ideas.

UNDERSTANDING KEY VOCABULARY

3 Match words (1–8) to definitions (a–h).

1 authenticity	a	the quality of being recently produced, grown or made
2 food miles		
3 a perfectionist	b	the main reason for buying something, or its best feature
4 freshness		
5 situated	c	a reduction in the usual price of something
6 to insist	d	the distance between where something is grown and where it is sold
7 a discount		
8 a selling point	e	someone who always wants everything to be correct
	f	located, found in
	g	say that something must happen
	h	when something is real, true or genuine

Turkish treats

Hello London foodies!

I'm kicking off this week's blog by talking about a fantastic new Turkish restaurant in Soho called Moda. I can't remember ever eating better dolma or hummus – it was so yummy! In fact, this is one of the things which the restaurant prides itself on – the freshness and authenticity of the ingredients. Apparently, the chef insists that the fruit and vegetables are brought over every day from his home region in Turkey – and from nowhere else. He may be a perfectionist, but it was so delicious that I can't complain. Moda isn't cheap, but it's definitely worth every penny.

And I've got great news for you. When I told him that I write a food blog, he said he'd give all my readers a 10% discount! Just mention this blog when you book.

A very different restaurant, where I had lunch last Monday, is Chez Fitz. Situated near Leicester Square, its main selling point is that its food is all locally sourced (within 30 kilometres of the restaurant). My friends and I were completely amazed – we had no idea that so much could be grown so close to central London. But it turns out that there are pockets of green all over the city – you just need to know where to look.

One final point: I couldn't believe how pricey my weekly shop was this week. Normally it's about £40, but this week it was more than £55 for more or less the same amount of food. Any ideas why?

More in a couple of weeks as I'm going away on my hols tomorrow!

COMMENTS

SouthLondonMum   10 October

Hi – regarding your last point, I've found the same thing recently. I read somewhere that the average 'shopping basket' has already increased by 20% this year. The prices have gone up so much, because of the awful weather we've been having, and they may go up even more. How are we meant to feed our families?

Ecovore   10 October

I'm not sure we should be supporting restaurants like Moda. They are very bad for the environment. What about all the extra carbon emissions from the 'food miles' created by bringing over those ingredients from Turkey?

Anonymous   11 October

I know what you're saying, Ecovore, but don't have a go at restaurants like Moda. If we grow exotic vegetables in the UK, then we have to use heated greenhouses and that probably uses even more energy.

WHILE READING

4 Read the blog again and answer the questions below.

   1 Why does the blog's author like Moda?

   2 What is the main selling point of Chez Fitz?

   3 What question does the blogger ask at the end of the article?

   4 What is 'SouthLondonMum' angry about?

READING FOR DETAIL

5 Read the blog again. Write true (T), false (F) or does not say (DNS) next to the statements below.

1 It is impossible to grow food in urban areas. _____
2 The author has noticed almost a 40% increase in the cost of food. _____
3 Restaurants like Chez Fitz will become more common in the future. _____
4 Chez Fitz tries to minimize food miles. _____
5 Food prices are going up in Turkey. _____
6 To eat at Moda regularly, you would have to be relatively wealthy. _____

6 The blog author uses informal language. Match informal words and phrases (1–6) to formal words (a–f). Use the context to help you.

1 kick off   a expensive
2 yummy   b holidays
3 pricey   c import
4 hols   d delicious
5 bring over   e criticize
6 have a go at   f begin

READING BETWEEN THE LINES

MAKING INFERENCES FROM THE TEXT

7 Work with a partner. Discuss the questions below.

1 Do you think the blog author likes *perfectionists*?
2 Why do you think the chef gave a discount to the blog's readers?
3 Why do you think the blogger's shopping was more expensive?

DISCUSSION

8 Work with a partner. Discuss the questions below.

1 What types of food are grown where you live? Are they eaten locally or are they sold elsewhere?
2 Should you believe restaurant reviews you read online? Why / Why not?
3 Do you read blogs or reviews online? Why / Why not?

READING 2

PREPARING TO READ

Good paragraphs in formal writing usually start with **topic sentences**. These tell you the subject of the paragraph. By reading the first sentence of each paragraph in a text, you can often get a good idea of the overall content and also which paragraph to look at if you need some specific information.

1   Read the topic sentences below. Work with a partner and discuss what you think the rest of each paragraph will be about.

   1   One country whose food has a long history of being 'globalized' is Italy.
   2   Food has always been very important for Italian families.
   3   Nowadays, however, Italian eating habits appear to have changed.
   4   On the plus side, globalization has increased the range of food available in Italy.
   5   In summary, globalization has had a significant influence on the way that Italians eat.

2   Skim read the essay and check your predictions.

What impact has globalization had on food and eating habits in Italy?

1   Globalization has significantly influenced food consumption in most parts of the world, but one country whose food has a long history of being 'globalized' is Italy. If you walk down any main street in any major world city, you will find at least one Italian restaurant. Furthermore, Italy has seen changes in its own eating habits due to influence from other countries. This essay will examine some of these changes and the issues they raise.

2   Food has always been very important for Italian families. Italians take a lot of pride in the making and preparation of food. Until recently, pasta – a basic Italian food – would have been made by people in their local area. Families would also have made the sauces to eat with the pasta at home. In addition, people's opportunity to experiment with foreign food was very limited, since only pizza and pasta were available in the local town square.

3   Nowadays, however, Italian eating habits appear to have changed. People no longer spend so much time preparing their meals. Indeed, frozen or takeaway Italian meals have become very popular in Italy. Furthermore, dried pasta is now mass-produced and is sold relatively cheaply in the supermarkets. Ready-made pasta sauces are also increasingly popular – sales have doubled in the last five years, according to one manufacturer. Another important change in Italian eating habits is the increasing popularity of foreign cuisine, especially Indian, Chinese and Japanese foods. This trend is more common in urban areas such as Rome, Milan and Venice, although many smaller towns are also experiencing similar changes.

4   These changes have both advantages and disadvantages. On the plus side, globalization has increased the range of food available in Italy. Italians now have much more choice in terms of what they eat. They also do not need to spend so long preparing and making food, unless of course they want to. In contrast, it can be argued that large restaurant chains are becoming increasingly powerful, resulting in the destruction of local and national specialities. Consequently, many Italians worry that they are losing their sense of nationality, as foreign food becomes more common.

5   In summary, globalization has had a significant influence on the way that Italians eat. Convenience foods have replaced many of the traditional home-cooked meals, and the availability of foreign foods has greatly increased. While this extra choice is welcomed by some, others fear the damage it may cause to Italian traditions. Possibly the global popularity of Italian food will ensure that it survives.

WHILE READING

3 Read the essay again. Do topics (1–7) below refer to the past, the present or both? Tick the correct column.

	past	present	both
1 mass production of pasta		✔	
2 domestic production of pasta			
3 lack of foreign food in Italy			
4 worldwide popularity of Italian food			
5 popularity of ready-made pasta sauces			
6 popularity of frozen food			
7 availability of Asian foods			

4 Complete the sentences below with your own words. Write between four and eight words for each sentence.

1 Italian restaurants can be found _____ .
2 In the past, Italians cooked _____ .
3 In Italian shops, you can now buy _____ .
4 Although recent changes mean Italians have more time and more choice, some dislike the fact that local food _____ .

READING BETWEEN THE LINES

5 Work with a partner. Discuss the questions below.

1 What types of reader do you think this essay is meant to appeal to?
   a people who have a general interest in food
   b people who are experts in Italian food
   c people who want to visit Italy on holiday
2 What do you think is the author's main intention in writing this essay?
   a to say that globalization has had a largely positive impact on Italian food
   b to say that globalization has damaged Italian culture
   c to say that globalization has fundamentally changed Italian food

DISCUSSION

6 Work with a partner. Discuss the questions below about your country.

1 What is the best-known national dish? Is it popular outside your country?
2 Is there a difference between the food that people eat in the countryside (or villages) and the food people eat in big cities?
3 Should governments stop the growth of multinational restaurant chains, to allow local, traditional restaurants to compete for customers?

◉ LANGUAGE DEVELOPMENT

EXPLANATION

Academic alternatives to phrasal verbs

When writing essays, it is important to use language which is more formal than you would use when speaking or in informal pieces of writing.

Phrasal verbs, which usually consist of a main verb followed by a particle (e.g. *up, on*), are less common in academic writing than in informal writing. In academic writing, phrasal verbs can often be replaced by a single word. Using these alternatives will make your writing seem more formal and academic.

1 Match phrasal verbs (1–9) to academic verbs (a–i).

1	go on	a	increase
2	go up	b	continue
3	turn down	c	study
4	look into	d	confuse
5	use up	e	remove
6	mix up	f	separate
7	leave out	g	refuse
8	take away	h	exclude
9	move apart	i	exhaust

2 Replace the phrasal verbs in bold with the correct form of the academic verbs (a–i) from Exercise 1.

1 The amount of migrant labour is expected to **go up**. _____

2 If multinational companies **go on** expanding, smaller local suppliers may die out. _____

3 Academics have been **looking into** the implications of globalization for many years. _____

4 Immigration can lead to people becoming **mixed up** about their sense of nationality. _____

5 Although many people benefit from globalization, others can also be **left out**. _____

6 Immigrants without suitable qualifications may have their visa requests **turned down**. _____

7 When a country's natural resources are **used up**, they may need to rely on other countries to supply them. _____

8 The need for workers from poor countries to seek work in rich countries can sometimes mean that families have to temporarily **move apart**. _____

9 Some supporters of global economic freedom believe that all trade barriers should be **taken away**. _____

GLOBALIZATION VOCABULARY

3 Complete the text about globalization with words from the box.

> farms   obesity   diet   monopoly   outlets   supermarkets
> consumption   poverty   multinational

There are both advantages and disadvantages of globalization in terms of food. On the negative side, (1)_____ companies have been criticized for opening too many fast-food (2)_____ in developing countries. This is causing (3)_____ in children, who are becoming addicted to a fatty westernized diet. Many of these companies are able to effectively set whatever price they like for the food because they have a (4)_____ . Therefore, they price their goods so they are cheaper than healthier local products and appeal to those people living in (5)_____ .

On the other hand, globalization means that people now have the possibility of more variety in their (6)_____ . The development of large-scale (7)_____ and fisheries means some products are more affordable and allow people to eat protein-rich foods on a regular basis for the first time. Large amounts of this food can often be bought cheaply by big (8)_____ and then sold to customers at a reasonable price. Because of these changes, (9)_____ of products such as meat has increased throughout the world.

CRITICAL THINKING

At the end of this unit, you will write the first draft of an essay. Look at this unit's writing task in the box below.

> How have food and eating habits changed in your country? Suggest some reasons for the changes.

Providing supporting examples

In academic writing, you need to justify and give supporting examples to any statements or opinions that you write, to show that they are true.

1 Read the statements below from the essay on page 21, and make a note of the examples given in the essay to support them.

   1 Italians take a lot of pride in the making and preparation of food.
   Supporting examples: _____

   _____

   2 People's opportunity to experiment with foreign food was very limited.
   Supporting examples: _____

   _____

   3 People no longer spend so much time preparing their meals.
   Supporting examples: _____

   _____

   4 Italians worry that they are losing their sense of nationality.
   Supporting examples: _____

   _____

   5 Globalization has become such a significant influence.
   Supporting examples: _____

   _____

Tables and diagrams can often help you to organize information that you can use to support your ideas in an essay.

2 Complete the table below about eating habits in your country.
Write two statements about the past and two about the present.
For each statement, write one supporting example.

APPLY

food and eating habits (past)		food and eating habits (now)	
statement	example	statement	example

WRITING

GRAMMAR FOR WRITING

Noun phrases

Nouns are often combined with other words to make noun phrases. These can express a more specific idea.

Noun phrases can be made by combining nouns with:

- other nouns: *building regulations*
- relative clauses: *a building which is very old*
- prepositional phrases: *the building at the back*
- adjectives: *the tall, white building*

In academic writing, many noun phrases are created by joining two nouns with *of*. These common phrases with *of* are used to talk about quantity: *a range of, a number of*.

1 Match the sets of noun phrases (1–4) to grammar structures (a–d).

1 world cuisine
  pasta sauces

2 people in their local area
  pride in the making and preparation of food
  a fact of modern life

3 large food chains
  ready-made pasta sauces
  major world city

4 the range of food which is available
  the type of food that people like
  a recent change which is unstoppable

a adjective + noun + noun

b noun + prepositional phrase

c noun phrase + relative clause

d noun + noun

2 Rearrange the words below to make noun phrases.

1 specialities / local _____ *local specialities* _____

2 a / list / dishes / of / traditional _____

3 programmes / cookery / television _____

4 allergies / and / increase / in / noticeable / a / diabetes

_____

5 a / of / fruits / variety / new _____

6 the / of / international / number / chefs _____

_____

7 different / the / cultures / impact / of _____

_____

8 preparation / time / a / of / deal / great / and _____

_____

UNL☉CK READING AND WRITING SKILLS 4

EXPLANATION

Time phrases

When talking about changes over a period of time, it is useful if you can use a range of time phrases in your academic writing. In academic writing, you are often expected to be precise about when something happened in the past.

3 Put the time phrases below in the correct part of the table, according to the period of time they refer to.

> around ten years ago   currently   in the past   historically
> in recent years   these days   at the present time   nowadays
> in the 1970s   formerly   presently   before the war
> in the eighteenth century

general past time	specific past time	present

4 Complete the sentences below about food in your country.

1 Nowadays, you can buy _____ .
2 In recent years, my country has seen many new types of restaurant, such as _____ .
3 Until the 1980s, it was impossible to find _____ .
4 These days, there are many _____ .
5 Around 20 years ago, you could not buy _____ .
6 Historically, people tended to live off _____ .
7 Presently, it is still not possible to get _____ .

ACADEMIC WRITING SKILLS

Essay types

There are many different types of academic essay. It is important to understand the particular style and characteristics expected of any essay you are writing, as this will help you structure it to present your argument effectively.

Defending an argument

In this type of essay, the writer gives an opinion at the beginning, and supports this argument throughout the essay. Arguments *against* the idea may also be mentioned, but the main purpose is to persuade the audience that the writer's argument is correct.

For and against

This type of essay is much more balanced. The writer sets out both advantages and disadvantages, before giving an opinion.

Problem–solution

A problem is outlined, and one or more solutions are described. The author justifies why one particular solution is the most appropriate.

Cause and effect

You may be asked to describe a situation and suggest what caused it. Alternatively, you may have to write about the effects something has had.

1 Match the essay titles below to the types of essay in the box above.

1 Should fast-food companies be allowed to aim their marketing at children?
2 Childhood obesity is a growing problem in many parts of the world. How can this be most effectively dealt with?
3 Outline the arguments given by supporters and critics of genetically modified food. Give your opinion on the issue.
4 In many countries, there has been a sharp rise in the amount of convenience food consumed. Why do you think this is?

Essay structure

Although there are different types of academic essay, the overall structure and principles tend to be the same.

Introduction

The first paragraph presents a general overview of what the piece of writing is going to be about and provides important background information.

Body paragraphs

These develop the main ideas outlined in the introduction and include relevant evidence and supporting information.

Conclusion

The last paragraph presents a short summary of the essay topic and the conclusions or recommendations of the writer.

2 Decide in which part of an essay you would probably find the examples below: the introduction, a body paragraph or the conclusion.

1 As we have seen, there is no simple solution for this problem ...
2 This essay will examine the advantages and disadvantages of ...
3 As for disadvantages, the most obvious one is ...
4 One possible solution is ...
5 An example of this can be seen in ...

UNL⭕CK READING AND WRITING SKILLS 4

WRITING TASK

> How have food and eating habits changed in your country?
> Suggest some reasons for the changes.

1 In the essay on page 21, each paragraph (1–5) has a different function. Match each paragraph to the functions below.

In the essay on page 21

a Description of changes _____   d Effects of changes _____
b Introduction _____   e Historical background _____
c Conclusion _____

2 Decide the function of each paragraph in your essay. Write the functions in column A.

	A	B
Paragraph 1		
Paragraph 2		
Paragraph 3		
Paragraph 4		
Paragraph 5		

3 Make notes in column B about what you are going to include in each paragraph.

4 Write the first draft of an essay. Use your essay plan above to help you structure your essay. Write 250–300 words.

EDIT

5 Use the task checklist to review your essay for content and structure.

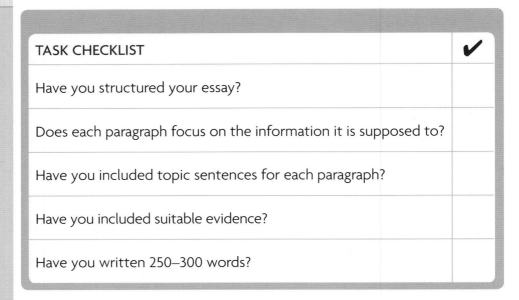

TASK CHECKLIST	✔
Have you structured your essay?	
Does each paragraph focus on the information it is supposed to?	
Have you included topic sentences for each paragraph?	
Have you included suitable evidence?	
Have you written 250–300 words?	

6 Make any necessary changes to your essay.

7 Now use the language checklist to edit your essay for language errors which are common to B2 learners.

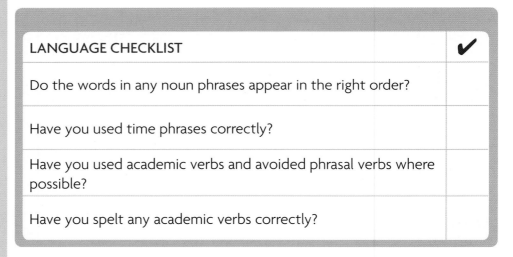

LANGUAGE CHECKLIST	✔
Do the words in any noun phrases appear in the right order?	
Have you used time phrases correctly?	
Have you used academic verbs and avoided phrasal verbs where possible?	
Have you spelt any academic verbs correctly?	

8 Make any necessary changes to your essay.

OBJECTIVES REVIEW

9 Check your objectives.

I can ...

watch and understand a
video about a world of
food in one city

very
well

not very
well

make predictions from
text types

very
well

not very
well

recognize essay types
and essay structures

very
well

not very
well

write the first draft of
an essay

very
well

not very
well

WORDLIST

UNIT VOCABULARY		ACADEMIC VOCABULARY	
authenticity (n)	IT communication (n)	at the moment (ph)	refuse (v)
chef (n)	labour (n)	at the present time	remove (v)
consumption (n)	monopoly (n)	(ph)	separate (v)
cooking equipment (n)	multinational (adj)	confuse (v)	these days (ph)
diet (n)	obesity (n)	continue (v)	
discount (n)	outlet (n)	currently (adv)	
ethnic group (n)	perfectionist (n)	exclude (v)	
food miles (n)	poverty (n)	exhaust (v)	
freshness (n)	prepared food (n)	formerly (adv)	
goods (n)	selling point (n)	historically (adv)	
industrialized (adj)	situated (adj)	increase (v/n)	
ingredient (n)	trade (n)	nowadays (adv)	
insist (v)		presently (adv)	

LEARNING OBJECTIVES

Watch and listen	Watch and understand a video about becoming a gondolier
Reading skills	Make inferences from a text
Academic writing skills	Write an introduction to an essay (1)
Writing task	Write an essay outlining the differences between two subjects

UNL⚙CK YOUR KNOWLEDGE

Work with a partner and ask and answer the questions below.

1 Describe the education system in your country. Talk about starting and leaving ages, different types of educational institutions and examinations.
2 Is there anything in that education system you would like to change? Give reasons.
3 Is it better to have a private or a state education? Give reasons.
4 What kinds of skill do you learn while working in a job? What skills do you learn from academic study? Which do you think you learn more skills from?

WATCH AND LISTEN

PREPARING TO WATCH

USING YOUR
KNOWLEDGE

1 Work in pairs. Answer the questions below about Venice.

1 Which country is Venice in?
2 Why do tourists go to Venice?
3 What kinds of jobs related to tourism do people do in Venice?

UNDERSTANDING
KEY VOCABULARY

2 Look at each group of three words below. Circle the word in each group with a different meaning.

1 difficult   challenging   (easy)
2 licence   ticket   permit
3 exam   test   discussion
4 apprentice   qualified   experienced
5 profession   hobby   job
6 distinctive   original   general

3 Complete each definition below with words from Exercise 2 which have a similar meaning.

1 If you are _____ or _____ , it means you have had the opportunity to learn the skills necessary for the job.
2 _____ and _____ are adjectives meaning 'requiring skill or effort'.
3 A _____ and a _____ both give their owners permission to do something.
4 If something is _____ or _____ , it is easily recognizable when compared to other things.
5 An _____ and a _____ are both ways to check whether someone has reached the appropriate skills level.
6 Your _____ or _____ is what you do to get paid and make a living.

WHILE WATCHING

4 You are going to watch a video about gondoliers. Do you think the
statements below are true or false?

1 Gondoliers are often female.
2 You are more likely to be a gondolier if one of your parents was one.
3 Gondoliers are a modern innovation for tourists.
4 It is a skilled job.
5 There is a long training period for gondoliers.
6 Gondoliers don't wear a uniform.

5 ▶ Watch the video and check your answers.

6 ▶ A student has taken the notes below about becoming a gondolier.
Find the mistakes in the notes and correct them. Watch the video again
to check your answers.

Before the exam
1 Candidates spend three years studying at university.
In the exam
2 Candidates are marked down if they go too fast.
3 Candidates should be particularly careful if there are low buildings.
After the exam
4 20–30 licences are awarded annually.
5 There are 425 gondoliers in Venice.
6 They wear stripy hats.

7 ▶ Work in pairs. Why do Venetians want to be gondoliers? Write four
reasons below. Watch again to check your answers.

1 _____
2 _____
3 _____
4 _____

8 Think about the four reasons for choosing to be a gondolier. To what
extent are these criteria important for your chosen career or studies?

DISCUSSION

9 Work with a partner. Discuss the questions below.

1 Why do you think the training for Venetian gondoliers is so difficult?
2 Which other jobs require a long training period? Why is that?
3 What sort of training is required for your career or future career?

PREPARING TO READ

1 Complete the table with the words from the box.

> academic course   lecture   vocational course
> tuition fees   face-to-face   seminar   module
> distance learning   scholarship   tutorial

elements of a university course	ways to deliver education	types of course	ways to pay for education
lecture	face-to-face		

2 Use the words in the table to complete the sentences below.

1 A _____ is an award that helps pay for a student's education, usually because of their academic achievement.

2 _____ learning is with a teacher, rather than by computer.

3 A _____ is a specific part of a whole course.

4 A _____ focuses on subjects which are linked to a particular job.

5 _____ focus more on the theory of subjects.

6 A _____ is a formal talk on an academic subject given to a large group of students.

7 _____ are payments made to cover the cost of an educational course.

8 A small group meeting with your teacher is a _____ .

9 Courses which are taken in an online environment are examples of _____ .

10 A _____ is when teachers and students discuss a topic in detail, on a one-to-one basis.

3 Work in pairs. Answer the questions below about your country or region.

1 What are popular academic courses at universities?
2 What kinds of vocational courses can you take in colleges?
3 How can students get help to pay their tuition fees?
4 How long does the English degree course last?
5 How are students assessed?

4 Read the web page and answer the questions in Exercise 3 about Middletown University.

Welcome to
Middletown University

Preparing you for success, whatever you want to do

Whether you are a national or an international student, we welcome you to Middletown University. Our reputation is built on providing high-quality education in both academic and vocational subjects. As well as priding ourselves on our traditional face-to-face learning, we have recently introduced a range of distance-learning courses.

OUR MOST POPULAR COURSES

Academic courses
Mathematics, English literature and History

Vocational courses
Engineering, Nursing, Accounting, Plumbing, Teaching and Catering

FREQUENTLY ASKED QUESTIONS

What kind of courses do you have?
Are you looking for a general academic course to increase your knowledge? Or do you need a vocational course to develop your skills for a specific profession? Or perhaps you need both. Whatever your academic and vocational needs, we are sure to have an appropriate course for you.

What do they cost?
Costs for our courses vary considerably. Click on each department's homepage for more information. Scholarships and bursaries are available for certain courses, particularly for those in the sciences and education.

SAMPLE COURSE OVERVIEW

BA in English Language and Literature

The main purpose of this course is to develop your ability to describe, analyze and manipulate features of the English Language, and to see how these are expressed in literature. As well as taking core modules which cover these areas, students will be able to specialize in their fields of interest.

Duration: three-year course

Course: Choose 12 out of 20 modules.

Weekly timetable: eight hours of lectures / four hours of seminars

Assessment: essays, exams and an 8,000-word dissertation at the end of the third year

Requirements: academic experience and interest in the subject; good school-exam grades

Diploma in teaching

In the first term, you will learn about the theory of teaching and how to be an effective teacher. In the second term, you will also begin teaching in a school. The third term is completely practical.

Duration: one-year course

Course: Choose six out of ten modules (three are compulsory).

Weekly timetable: six hours of lectures / two hours of seminars / six hours of classroom teaching

Assessment: combination of essays and classroom observation

Requirement: first degree in specific subject area

LATEST NEWS
- Apprenticeship opportunities now available with local businesses including carpenters, electricians and plumbers
- New part-time job opportunities available for undergraduates/graduates

WHILE READING

5 Read the web page again. Are the statements below true (T), false (F) or the web page does not say (DNS)?

1 Only face-to-face learning opportunities are available. _____

2 There is one fee for all courses. _____

3 More than 30 different courses are available. _____

4 Courses are assessed in different ways. _____

5 Essays and dissertations must be written on a computer. _____

6 To access the BA English course, you need to have passed school examinations. _____

7 A teaching diploma involves learning theory in the second term. _____

8 Students can choose any of the modules on the teaching diploma course. _____

9 There are opportunities for part-time jobs at Middletown University. _____

READING BETWEEN THE LINES

Sometimes, writers suggest the meaning of something without saying it directly. Being able to read this inferred meaning (as well as the literal meaning of the words) is a useful skill. Practise using reasoning, logic and your knowledge of the world to work out the real meaning behind the words you read.

6 Work with a partner. Discuss the questions below.

1 Why do the costs for courses at Middletown University vary considerably?

2 Why do you think there are state scholarships for science and education courses?

3 On the BA course, what kind of topics could you write about for your dissertation?

4 Why are there some 'core' modules which are compulsory, and others that you can choose?

5 Why aren't there any exams for the Diploma?

DISCUSSION

7 Work with a partner. Discuss the questions below.

1 What kind of study or training would you like to do in the future?

2 Should universities be free for students? Why / Why not?

3 Is it useful to study academic subjects like Philosophy or History, which may not directly lead to a job?

READING 2

PREPARING TO READ

1 Match collocations (1–9) with their meanings (a–i).

1	modern phenomenon	a	key values
2	distance learning	b	electronic communication
3	technological advances	c	individual connection
4	credible alternative	d	online college
5	virtual university	e	reliable substitute
6	core principles	f	recent trend
7	personal relationship	g	important distinction
8	online conversations	h	online course
9	significant difference	i	scientific developments

2 Look at the statements below. Do you think they are true (T) or false (F)?

1 Distance learning is a new idea. _____

2 It has been possible to get a university degree online in America since the 1980s. _____

3 Distance learning requires good technological access. _____

4 Distance learning is very personal. _____

5 Students generally enjoy meeting face-to-face with other people on their course. _____

6 Face-to-face learning is better than distance learning. _____

3 Read the article on the next page and check your answers to Exercise 2.

WHILE READING

4 Match paragraph descriptions (1–5) to the correct paragraphs (A–E) in the article.

1 Knowledge transfer _____

2 General summary and conclusions _____

3 Instructor–pupil interaction _____

4 The history and background of the topic _____

5 Peer-to-peer contact _____

Distance or face-to-face learning – what's the difference?

A Although many people think it is a modern phenomenon, distance learning has been around for at least 200 years in one form or another. Historical examples of long-distance learning include students being sent a series of weekly lessons by post. The technological advances of the past 20 or so years, however, have meant that this form of education is now able to rival face-to-face learning as a credible alternative. Indeed, 1996 saw the establishment of the world's first 'virtual university' in the United States, showing how far distance learning has come in a relatively short space of time.

B When comparing the two systems, the first and most obvious area to focus on is the way that learning is delivered. Distance learning is heavily dependent on technology, particularly the internet. On a face-to-face course, students may only require a computer for the purpose of writing an essay. In comparison, when learning remotely, technology is the principal means of communication. The flexibility this provides means that students may be better able to learn at their own pace, following their own timetable, but it may also mean that learners have to be well-organized and self-disciplined. They must therefore be highly motivated in order to do well on the distance-learning courses.

C In terms of the teacher–student relationship, the core principles remain the same. Namely, the teacher is the 'knower', and is responsible for helping students understand the key components of the course. However, the nature of the relationship may differ slightly within the two modes of delivery. With face-to-face learning, the teacher and student have the opportunity to develop a personal relationship through lectures, seminars and tutorials. This is different from a distance-learning course, where the teacher may seldom or indeed never actually meet the student. This may make it hard for teachers to understand their learners' specific learning needs.

D For many students, interaction with their peers is one of the best aspects of university education. Generally, students like to meet regularly and talk to people on the same course. However, this kind of interaction on a distance-learning course is less common. Although people can increasingly interact through online conversations and messageboards, there is a significant difference between virtual and real interaction. Time and geography must also be considered when contrasting these two types of learning. Face-to-face learning must take place in real-time and in one location. Conversely, distance learning can happen at any time and in any location, since the learning is not restricted by geography.

E In conclusion, it is difficult to state whether one form of learning is better than another, as they cater for different audiences. What is important to understand is the different ways in which they operate, and that there are strong similarities between the two systems, which can both produce positive results.

5 Tick the correct parts of the table. Are statements (1–5) about distance learning, face-to-face learning or both?

	distance learning	face-to-face learning	both
1 develops a strong student–teacher relationship		✔	
2 heavily reliant on technology			
3 flexible with time			
4 students can interact with each other in person			
5 can be effective ways of teaching			
6 requires a high level of motivation			
7 not limited by geography			
8 can suit many types of students			

READING BETWEEN THE LINES

6 Work with a partner. Answer the questions below, based on information in the article.

1 Why do some people think distance learning is a modern idea?
2 Why can online learning be slightly impersonal?
3 Why do students often like to meet other people on the same course?
4 Does the author of the article generally approve or disapprove of distance learning?

DISCUSSION

7 Work with a partner. Discuss the questions below.

1 Have you ever tried to learn something online? What were the advantages and disadvantages of doing this?
2 Are there any problems with face-to-face teaching?
3 How do you think teaching will change in the future?
4 Will distance learning become the most common kind of teaching in the future?

⊙ LANGUAGE DEVELOPMENT

EDUCATION VOCABULARY

1 Complete each sentence below with a word from the box. Use the Glossary on page 195 to help you.

> assignment   journal   examination   plagiarism   term
> lecturer   tutor   dissertation   semester

1 The word for a written essay at university is an _____ .
2 A timed assessment under silent conditions is an _____ .
3 An academic year can be split into three periods, each called a

 _____ .
4 An academic year can also be divided into two periods, each called a

 _____ .
5 _____ is when students copy from, or do not acknowledge, their sources when writing an essay.
6 A _____ is a quarterly peer-reviewed collection of research papers.
7 A _____ is a long essay of between 8,000 and 12,000 words.
8 A _____ is the holder of a research position at a university who also teaches.
9 A _____ assumes responsibility for students' academic and personal welfare.

ACADEMIC WORDS

2 Match academic words (1–11) to definitions (a–k).

1	alternative	a	the foundation or starting of an organization
2	establishment	b	parts or features of something
3	virtual	c	enthusiasm for doing something
4	significant	d	different from something else
5	core	e	particular or exact
6	a principle	f	existing in a technological environment
7	a component	g	communication between things or people
8	interaction	h	important or noticeable
9	motivation	i	the most important part of something
10	aspects	j	a part which makes up something bigger
11	specific	k	a basic idea or rule

3 Complete the sentences below with the correct form of some of the words from Exercise 2.

1 Many students prefer to study a vocational subject as an _____ to an academic course.
2 For many students, _____ with their peers is important.
3 One of the best _____ of university education is meeting the other students on the course.
4 Tutors help their students understand the key _____ of their course.
5 Distance learning requires a high level of _____ .
6 Distance learning can make it hard for teachers to understand students' _____ learning needs.
7 As well as taking _____ modules, students will be able to specialize in their areas of interest.
8 1996 saw the establishment of the world's first _____ university, which operated only on the internet.

CRITICAL THINKING

At the end of this unit, you will write an essay outlining the differences between two subjects. Look at this unit's writing task in the box below.

> Outline the various differences between studying a language and studying mathematics. In what ways may they in fact be similar?

ANALYZE

1 Use a dictionary to check your understanding of the subjects below. Write them in the Venn diagram, according to whether they are academic or vocational subjects, or both.

> Hairdressing   Philosophy   Beauty Therapy
> Golf Course Management   Law   Business Administration
> Art History   Catering   Mathematics   Biochemistry
> Electrical Engineering   Medicine   Construction
> Computer Science

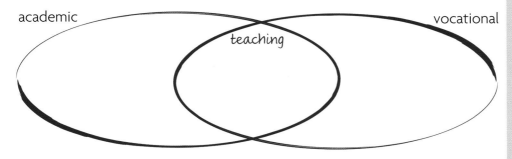

academic   vocational

teaching

2 Add more subjects to the Venn diagram. Look at Reading 1 again if you need more ideas.

3 Look at the students' opinions below. Which are in favour of vocational courses and which are in favour of academic subjects?

1 People shouldn't have to focus on a specific career until they leave university; they should focus on gaining subject knowledge.

2 You need the correct qualifications and skills for the career you want to follow.

3 Degrees in subjects like Art History are a waste of money and you won't get a good job at the end.

4 Yes, you will be able to earn a lot of money with a Law degree but you don't have to study it for three years. You can do a post-graduate qualification and combine it with another degree.

5 With a practical qualification, you learn real-world skills and get work experience. It makes you more employable overall.

6 There are lots of transferable skills from studying an academic subject. It's a good grounding for many careers.

4 Discuss the questions below with a partner.

    1 Is it better to study an academic subject or a vocational course?

    2 Why do you think Law, Medicine and Computer Science are the most popular subjects at British universities and colleges?

WRITING

GRAMMAR FOR WRITING

EXPLANATION

Comparison and contrast language

The ability to compare ideas which are similar (or contrast ideas which are different) is an important skill in writing, especially when we are asked to discuss a subject before we give our opinion.

Comparison

University students on face-to-face courses usually have contact with their tutors every week. **Similarly,** students doing distance-learning courses will get in touch with their tutors in online forums every week.

Contrast

Universities charge high tuition fees for academic subjects. **However,** colleges charge much less for vocational courses.

1 Which phrases below introduce a comparison between two similar ideas? Which introduce a contrast between two different ideas?

    1 In contrast, ...

    2 In the same way, ...

    3 Conversely, ...

    4 Likewise, ...

2 Complete the sentences below with your own ideas.

1 Academic subjects like Law lead to high-flying careers. In contrast, _____

_____

_____

2 Medicine involves both academic and vocational aspects. Similarly, _____

_____

_____

3 Theoretical courses tend not to prepare students for the real world.
Conversely, _____

_____

4 Practical hands-on courses are expensive. Likewise, _____

_____

_____

EXPLANATION

Comparison and contrast language in topic sentences

There are a number of ways to show comparison and contrast in essays, usually
in the topic sentences of paragraphs. These are usually longer and use different
types of punctuation.

- Teachers **and** parents **are similar in that they both** have the child's interests at heart.
- Teachers **and** parents **are different in that they** may not have the same expectations of the child.
- Colleges, **like** universities, charge tuition fees.
- Colleges, **unlike** universities, specialize in vocational courses.
- **The main difference between** teachers **and** parents **is that** teachers are paid, **whereas** parents are not.
- **The main similarity between** teachers **and** parents **is that they both** want the best for the child.

3 Match the topic sentence halves.

1 Academic courses and vocational subjects are similar
2 Academic courses, like vocational subjects,
3 Academic courses and vocational subjects are different
4 Academic courses, unlike vocational subjects,
5 The main difference between academic and vocational subjects
6 The main similarity between academic and vocational subjects

a lead to very useful qualifications.
b is that they both allow students to learn new skills.
c is that academic courses are theoretical whereas vocational subjects
   are not.
d in that they both charge tuition fees.
e in that they do not have the same admission grades.
f offer a career in academic research for the best graduates.

ACADEMIC WRITING SKILLS

Analyzing an essay question

Some essay questions can seem complicated, but they are actually quite simple. Analyzing a question by breaking it down into smaller elements and identifying the key vocabulary can help to simplify the task.

> Discuss the extent and the nature of the influence that technology has had on education in the past 20 years.

1 Highlight the key words or phrases: *influence, technology, education.*
2 Highlight any words or phrases which limit what you should write about: *in the past 20 years.*
3 Highlight any task words (words that tell you what you have to do): *Discuss the extent and the nature ...*

1 Look at writing task A below and compare it with version B. Do they have the same meaning?

> A Outline the various differences between theoretical study and the practical development of employment skills. In what ways may they in fact be similar?
>
> B Describe the similarities and differences between academic study and vocational training.

2 Look at these phrases from writing task A. Find phrases in writing task B that have a similar meaning.

1 outline the various differences between _____
2 theoretical study _____
3 the practical development of employment skills _____
4 In what ways may they, in fact, be similar? _____

Writing an introduction to an essay (1)

An essay introduction tells the reader what your essay will contain. For example:

- Background information, context or the reason why this subject is important: *The birth of many new forms of technology in the past two decades has ...*
- The aim of the essay: *This essay will discuss/examine/outline/analyze ...*
- An outline, or map, of the essay: *First, ... Next, ... Finally, ...*

A good introduction should:

- be written in your own words (do not repeat the words in the essay title)
- be general (do not write about yourself, unless the essay asks for this)
- refer to all parts of the essay question
- be focused on the essay question (do not add any unnecessary information).

3 Which essay introductions below follow the advice in the box? What are the problems with the other introductions?

1 This essay will outline the various differences between theoretical study and the practical development of employment skills and say in what ways they may in fact be similar.

2 Academic study is far more important than vocational training. This essay will discuss how academic study is the best way to get a good career and better station in life.

3 Have you always wondered about the differences between theoretical study and vocational training? I think it's really important to try both to get a fantastic job after uni, actually.

4 On the face of it, vocational education and academic study have little in common. Academic study promotes the discussion of ideas while vocational education provides a useful way into a career. However this essay will describe how both educational sectors have a number of similarities as well as their obvious differences. I will conclude by suggesting that a mixture of practice and theory often produces the best courses for students.

5 Universities are important to the economy of the country but many other things are also important to the economy, like trade and natural resources. However, every coin has two sides and practical skills are also important to the economy because the job market requires these valuable skills.

6 I used to go to college when I was 18 and I had a great time learning graphic design. The course was very good for my career and today my job is in that line. However, I can see the advantages of a university degree. My brother went to university to learn Art History and he has a good job at an advertising company so you never know how useful these things can be in the future.

WRITING TASK

> Outline the various differences between studying a language and studying mathematics. In what ways may they in fact be similar?

1 Work in groups. Make a list of the features of studying a language and the features of studying mathematics. Write them in the appropriate sections of a Venn diagram like the one below.

PLAN AND WRITE
A FIRST DRAFT

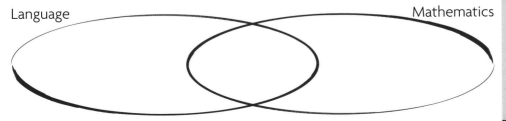

Language   Mathematics

2 Plan your essay. Make notes in the table below.

Paragraph 1: introduction	
Paragraph 2: body (differences)	
Paragraph 3: body (similarities)	
Paragraph 4: conclusion	

3 Write your essay using the plan. Write 250–300 words.

4 Use the task checklist to review your essay for content and structure.

TASK CHECKLIST	✔
Have you given background information in your introduction?	
Does your introduction focus on the essay question?	
Does your introduction refer to all parts of the essay question?	
Have you used examples to strengthen your arguments in the body paragraphs?	
Have you included a relevant conclusion?	
Have you written 250–300 words?	

5 Make any necessary changes to your essay.

6 Now use the language checklist opposite to edit your essay for language errors which are common to B2 learners.

7 Make any necessary changes to your essay.

LANGUAGE CHECKLIST	✔
Have you used comparison and contrast language correctly?	
Have you used a range of academic words?	
Have you included collocations correctly?	

OBJECTIVES REVIEW

8 Check your objectives.

I can ...

watch and understand a
video about becoming
a gondolier

very   not very
well   well

make inferences from a
text

very   not very
well   well

write an introduction to
an essay

very   not very
well   well

write an essay outlining
the differences between
two subjects

very   not very
well   well

WORDLIST

UNIT VOCABULARY		ACADEMIC VOCABULARY	
apprentice (n)	plagiarism (n)	alternative (n)	principle (n)
assignment (n)	profession (n)	aspect (n)	significant (adj)
dissertation (n)	scholarship (n)	component (n)	specific (adj)
examination (n)	semester (n)	establishment (n)	virtual (adj)
face-to-face (adj)	seminar (n)	interaction (n)	
journal (n)	term (n)	motivation (n)	
lecture (n)	tuition fee (n)		
lecturer (n)	tutor (n)		
licence (n)	tutorial (n)		
module (n)	vocational course (n)		

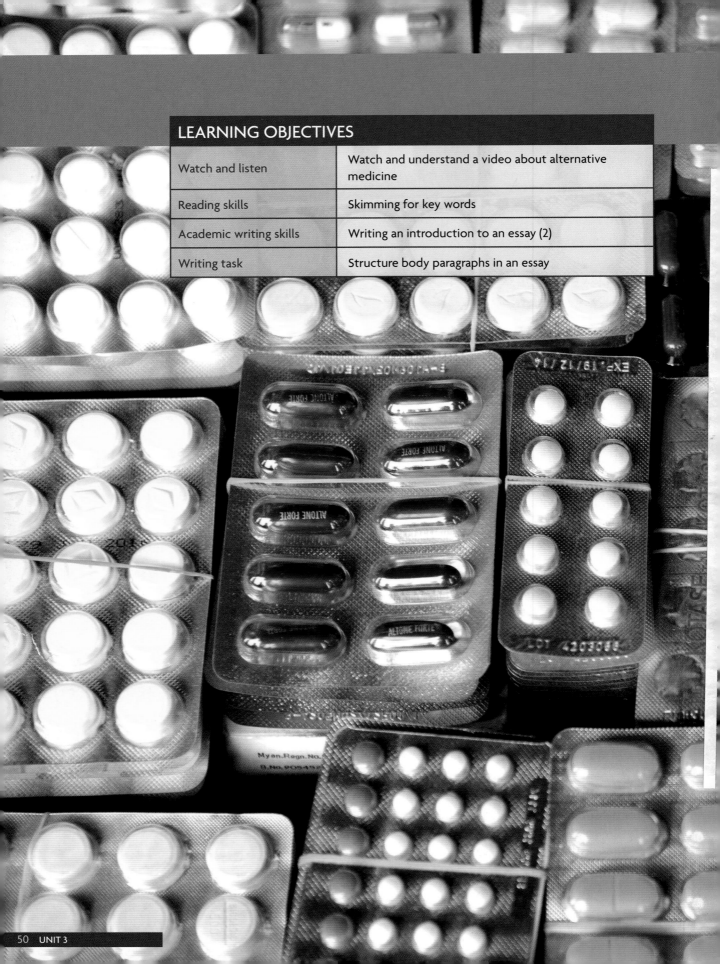

LEARNING OBJECTIVES

Watch and listen	Watch and understand a video about alternative medicine
Reading skills	Skimming for key words
Academic writing skills	Writing an introduction to an essay (2)
Writing task	Structure body paragraphs in an essay

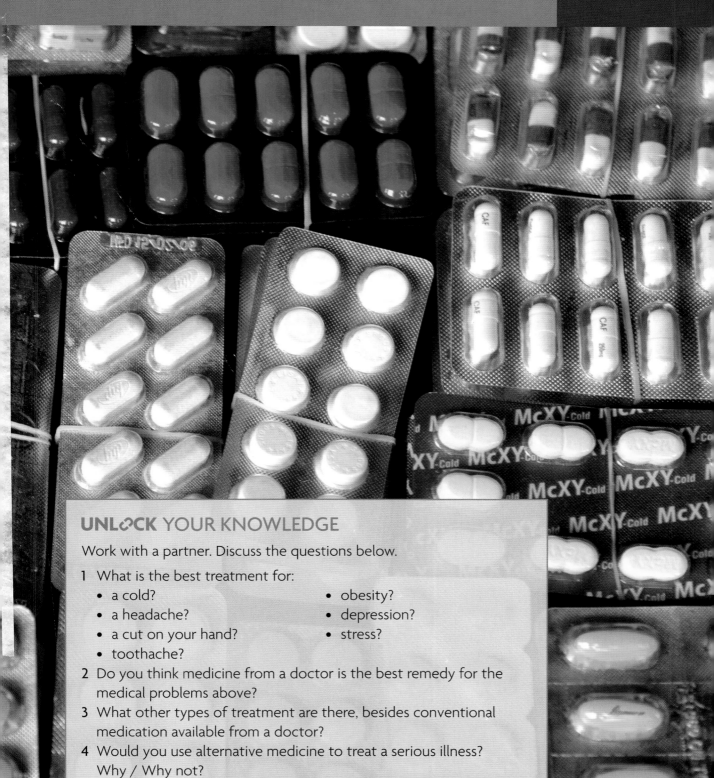

UNL⊙CK YOUR KNOWLEDGE

Work with a partner. Discuss the questions below.

1 What is the best treatment for:
    - a cold?
    - a headache?
    - a cut on your hand?
    - toothache?
    - obesity?
    - depression?
    - stress?

2 Do you think medicine from a doctor is the best remedy for the medical problems above?

3 What other types of treatment are there, besides conventional medication available from a doctor?

4 Would you use alternative medicine to treat a serious illness? Why / Why not?

WATCH AND LISTEN

PREPARING TO WATCH

UNDERSTANDING
KEY VOCABULARY

1 Look at the pairs of words below. Tick the pairs which you think are *synonyms* (i.e. which have roughly the same meaning).

1 remedies / treatments
2 alternative health centres / hospitals
3 disease / illness
4 natural / synthetic
5 globe / world

2 Work in pairs. Discuss the difference in meaning between the words in Exercise 1 that are not synonyms.

USING VISUALS TO
PREDICT CONTENT

3 Work with a partner. Look at the photos and decide what kind of medicine/treatment you think will be the focus of the video.

4 Which of the statements below do you think are true?

1 Traditional forms of medicine are popular throughout the world, as well as in their country of origin.
2 Many modern medicines are based on plants.
3 Traditional forms of medicine are completely safe.

5 ▶ Watch the video and check your answers.

WHILE WATCHING

LISTENING FOR KEY
INFORMATION

6 ▶ Watch the video again. Are the statements below true (T) or false (F)?

1 Other medicines are older than Ayurveda.   _____
2 'Ayurveda' can be translated as 'the science of long life'.   _____
3 It was invented nearly 3,500 years ago.   _____
4 There are more than a quarter of a million Ayurvedic doctors in India.   _____
5 Any treatment which uses plants is called 'Ayurvedic'.   _____
6 Some scientists have concerns about natural medicine.   _____

7 Give an example of the things below which are mentioned in the video.

1 a common painkiller
2 a heavy metal
3 a place where plants are commonly used to treat diseases
4 a natural ingredient

8 Match the note-taking symbols and abbreviations (1–7) with their meaning (a–g).

1 >   a compared with
2 &   b number
3 cf   c more than
4 e.g.   d including/include
5 /   e for example
6 inc.   f and
7 #   g or

9 Rewrite the notes below as full sentences.

1 Ayurveda > 3,500 yrs old & # of doctors > 300,000

_____

_____

2 plants used in Ayurveda cf other places – e.g. Peru/Serengeti

_____

_____

3 some medicines inc. metals, e.g. lead/mercury

_____

_____

10 ▶ Work in pairs. Watch the video without sound. Imagine you are the narrator of the video. Decide what you would say.

RESPONDING TO THE
VIDEO CONTENT

DISCUSSION

11 Work with a partner. Discuss the questions below.

1 How do you feel about the medicines in the video?
2 If you get ill in your country, where do you go for treatment?
3 Has medical treatment in your country changed much over the past 25 years?

PREPARING TO READ

Many texts you read will have words you do not know, especially if you are reading about a specialist subject. You could prepare yourself for reading by skimming the title and the introduction paragraph for any unknown words. Try to decide from the context whether these words are important to understand or not. If they are, try to guess their meaning or check them in a dictionary.

SKIMMING FOR KEY WORDS

1 Skim the title and introduction of the article and underline the words from the box.

> dilute   homeopathy   drug   proponent   debate   critic
> controversial   fund

2 Decide which statement below (1–4) best describes the main idea of the article.

1 The article presents the arguments for and against conventional medicine.
2 The article discusses whether an alternative medical treatment should be free for patients.
3 The article gives two people's opinions on the effectiveness of homeopathy.
4 The article discusses a range of alternative medical treatments.

3 Match the words in the box above to the correct definition. Use a dictionary to help you.

1 a system of treating diseases in which ill people are given very small amounts of natural substances
2 to make a liquid weaker by mixing in something else
3 to provide the money to pay for an event, activity or organization
4 any natural or artificially made chemical that is used as a medicine
5 a person who speaks publicly in support of a particular idea or plan of action
6 a serious discussion of a subject in which many people take part
7 a person who says that they do not approve of someone or something
8 causing disagreement or discussion

The homeopathy debate

Most national health systems use conventional medicine, meaning that illnesses are treated using drugs and surgery. However, there is also a range of alternative medical treatments to choose from. One controversial treatment is homeopathy, where patients are given highly diluted mixtures of natural substances. Supporters of homeopathy believe that people should have a choice in the type of treatment they receive, whereas others argue that homeopathy does not work and therefore should not be funded by the state. Here, one proponent and one critic present their cases.

Homeopathy should be state funded

by Abigail Hayes (Professional homeopath)

The British National Health Service was founded to provide free healthcare to people who need it. Since it was founded in 1948, patients have been able to get homeopathic treatment, and there's no good reason why this shouldn't continue. Most importantly, it's estimated that homeopathic treatments only cost the NHS between £4–10 million a year. This is a fraction of the cost paid out to conventional drug companies. Also, but perhaps less importantly, over 400 doctors regularly recommend homeopathic treatments. Since they are cheap and popular, I find it difficult to understand why the government is considering cutting funding for them. Why shouldn't people be allowed to make their own health choices? They have this freedom in other aspects of their lives – for example which school to send their children to – so why not in terms of their healthcare?

As for the critics who argue that homeopathy doesn't work, I could give hundreds of examples of patients who have been cured by my treatment. On top of that, there's plenty of research which shows the benefits it can bring. Homeopathy wouldn't have survived so long if it was complete nonsense. It has much more than just a placebo effect. Too much emphasis is sometimes put on providing 'proof' of why something works. Belief is just as powerful.

Homeopathy should not be state funded

by Dr. Piers Wehner (NHS General Practitioner)

We don't really know whether homeopathy helps people feel better because of the remedies themselves or because people believe they will work. Some people just feel better when they get personal care and attention from their homeopathic practitioner. For me and many others in my profession, there is absolutely no proof that says homeopathic treatment works. The government's chief scientist confirmed this when he said there was 'no real evidence' to support homeopathy. We live in difficult economic times and every penny the government spends should be checked to ensure that it is not wasted. In fact, 75% of British doctors are against the state funding of homeopathy.

One of the main arguments put forward by supporters of homeopathy is that this therapy doesn't cause any damage. However, people may think they are treating their illness by taking homeopathic remedies when there is actually no scientific evidence that this is true. Even more seriously, patients who rely on homeopathy alone for treating life-threatening illnesses like cancer could be taking a big risk. The cancer might no longer be treatable by proven methods if the patient has wasted too long trying homeopathy. This can cost lives.

WHILE READING

4 Read the article and say whether the statements below are true (T), false (F) or the article does not say (DNS).

1 The majority of countries use alternative rather than conventional medicine. _____

2 Homeopathy is currently available through the British National Health Service. _____

3 In the UK, people currently have a choice as to what treatment they can get. _____

4 More than two-thirds of doctors in Britain are against homeopathy. _____

5 Traditional Indian doctors frequently used homeopathic remedies. _____

6 The British National Health Service was established within the last 50 years. _____

7 Homeopathy is the only type of healthcare available in the US. _____

8 Weak, diluted liquids are a common form of homeopathic treatment. _____

5 Which of the two people in the article would agree with the statements below?

	Abigail Hayes	Piers Wehner
1 The doctor says it's too late to help her now. If only she'd gone to see him earlier.		
2 Look, if I don't want to risk the side effects of drugs, why should I have to?		
3 When I see proper clinical trials that prove the effectiveness of homeopathy, *then* I'll change my mind.		
4 The mind has incredibly strong healing powers.		
5 If it means we could stop paying all that money to drug companies, then I'm for it.		
6 It worked. I don't know why. It doesn't seem possible but I'm just happy that it worked.		
7 This is serious. You've got to see a doctor. You can keep taking the homeopathic treatment as well, if you want.		
8 If three-quarters of professionals are against it, I'm against it.		

READING BETWEEN THE LINES

6 Work with a partner. Discuss possible reasons for the statements below.

1 Homeopathic treatment is much cheaper than conventional medicine.
2 The government is considering cutting funding for homeopathy.
3 Belief is as powerful as medicine.
4 Personal care and attention make people feel better.
5 There is no real proof that homeopathy works.
6 Doctors need to see scientific evidence.

DISCUSSION

7 Work with a partner. Discuss the questions below.

1 Why do you think alternative medicines are popular with some people?
2 Should alternative medicines like homeopathy be funded by the government?
3 Do you think alternative medicine only creates a 'placebo effect'?

READING 2

PREPARING TO READ

1 Complete the sentences with the correct words from the box.

> labour costs   premium   burden   regardless   deducted
> consultation   treatment   safety net

1 A _____ is something difficult or unpleasant that you have to deal with or worry about.
2 After three months of _____ , the patient can now walk well.
3 Everybody must pay their share, _____ of how much they earn.
4 It is a good idea to save some money as a _____ , just in case you lose your job.
5 The doctor examined me when I went to him for a _____ .
6 The money you owe the company will be _____ from your salary.
7 When you calculate the price of constructing a building, you have to consider materials and _____ .
8 You have to pay an insurance _____ every month.

2 Work with a partner. Answer the questions below.

1 Do you have to pay for healthcare in your country?
2 What healthcare provision, if any, does your government pay for?
3 Should everybody be able to access free healthcare?
4 How should healthcare be funded – privately or by the state?

3 Read an essay about three systems of healthcare provision. Answer the questions.

1 Which system is most similar to the one your country follows? Are there any differences?

2 Which system most closely matches your answers to questions 3 and 4 in Exercise 2?

Should healthcare be free?

Who pays for healthcare? The answer varies from country to country. While in some nations it is completely free for all residents, in others you can only see a doctor if you pay. This essay will identify three main models of healthcare throughout the world, noting some advantages and disadvantages of each.

1 Free or public healthcare

There are several systems within this model, but they all aim to provide free basic healthcare. In some countries, consultations, treatment and medicines are free to all citizens. This may be paid for directly by the government, perhaps funded by the country's valuable natural resources which the government owns. Other countries collect money from citizens through taxes based on their income. Workers pay according to how much they earn and employers also make a contribution. Hospitals and other medical services are then provided and run by the government. There may also be some private medical services that people can choose to buy. The advantage of systems such as these is clear: free basic healthcare for all, regardless of income. However, it is a very expensive system and, as life expectancy and costs rise, many countries are facing either an unsustainable financial burden, or a drop in the quality of services and facilities provided.

2 Private healthcare

In the private model, healthcare is only available to patients who pay for it and healthcare providers are commercial companies. In wealthier countries, most citizens take out health insurance to cover their potential medical costs. However, not everyone can afford this, and some governments have a scheme which gives financial assistance to those who need urgent medical care but are unable to afford it. In other nations, there is no such safety net, and those who cannot pay simply do not get the healthcare they need, unless they can get help. The disadvantages of this system are obvious: not only are individuals deprived of the medical attention they need, but also the lack of preventative medicine

means that infectious diseases can quickly spread. One advantage, however, is that a higher quality of care provision can sometimes be maintained by commercial organizations than by struggling government-funded ones.

3 A mixed system

In many countries, there is a mix of public and private funding. This system requires all its citizens to take out health insurance. This is deducted from salaries by the employer, who also has to make a contribution for each worker. Citizens are able to choose their healthcare providers, which may be public or private. However, in some systems, private companies are not permitted to make a profit from providing basic healthcare. This model provides more flexibility than either the public or private models, and ensures access to healthcare for all. However, it has been criticized for driving up labour costs, which can lead to unemployment.

Conclusion

This essay has examined three models of healthcare provision and some advantages and disadvantages of each. As no system is perfect, several countries are now considering a combination of the models for their national health system. The challenge is to find a system which provides a good level of healthcare to all citizens, but which is also affordable and practical.

WHILE READING

4 Read the essay again. Identify which system (1–3) in the essay the countries below use.

1 **The UK**. Under this country's National Health Service, all workers pay National Insurance according to how much they earn. This is collected by the government and is used to pay for hospitals and other medical treatment. This is all free, except for prescriptions. Most hospitals are owned and run by the government.

2 **The Democratic Republic of Congo**. Here, many people do not have access to a doctor. Even those who do manage to see one often cannot afford the treatment.

3 **Qatar**. This country spends more on healthcare per person than any other country in the Gulf region. Healthcare is free (or almost free) for everyone. This is paid for by the government.

4 **The US**. Here, healthcare is expensive. About 40% of people have no health insurance.

5 **Germany.** Here, most workers have to pay health insurance from their salaries.

5 Scan the essay quickly to find words to complete the table below.

synonyms of *people*	
synonyms of *money*	
related to *healthcare*	

READING BETWEEN THE LINES

6 Decide which statement (a or b) best describes the views and structure of the essay.

1 a The author writes in favour of one system.
  b The author presents a balanced view of the different systems.
2 a The essay provides a brief outline of the systems.
  b The essay gives details of the systems.

DISCUSSION

7 Work with a partner. Discuss the questions below.

1 Why do you think different countries have different healthcare systems?
2 Should governments provide the following services free to citizens: water, electricity, use of roads, refuse collection?
3 Which countries do you think have the best healthcare – those with free or those with private systems?

MEDICAL VOCABULARY

1 Match words and phrases (1–7) with definitions (a–g).

1 disease epidemic	**a** the official legal right to make or sell an invention for a particular number of years
2 sedentary lifestyle	
3 patent	**b** a disease which can be avoided, often by a person looking after themselves better
4 underfunding	
5 preventable illness	**c** lack of money provided for something, often academic or scientific research
6 cosmetic surgery	
7 drug dependency	**d** an illness which affects large numbers of people at the same time
	e a medical operation which is intended to improve a person's appearance
	f a way of life which does not involve much activity or exercise
	g being unable to function normally without a particular medicine

2 Complete the sentences below with the correct form of words and phrases from Exercise 1.

1 Following a national emergency, such as an earthquake, clean water must be restored quickly to prevent the spread of a
_____ .

2 Less spending by the government means hospitals suffer from
_____ .

3 _____ can occur when people are prescribed a medicine for a long time.

4 The rise in obesity, particularly among young people, is often the result of a more _____ .

5 A lack of exercise and eating the wrong food can lead to the development of a _____ such as diabetes.

6 Pharmaceutical companies take out _____ on their new drugs, but once these have expired, other companies can manufacture and market them.

7 Some people travel abroad for expensive medical treatment or change their appearance through _____ .

ACADEMIC VOCABULARY

3 Write the correct adjective forms of the academic nouns in the table.

	adjective	definition	noun
1		having a negative or harmful effect on something	adversity
2		having the qualities that you connect with trained and skilled people	profession
3		against the law	illegality
4		connected with the body	physicality
5		difficult to understand or find an answer to because of having many different parts	complexity
6		enough or satisfactory for a particular purpose	adequacy
7		traditional and ordinary	convention
8		exact and accurate	precision
9		related to the treatment of illness and injuries	medicine

4 Choose the correct answer.

1 Many countries are fighting against the growing use of *complex/illegal* drugs.

2 Doctors and nurses are two examples of *precision/professional* healthcare practitioners.

3 People have the right to expect an *illegal/adequate* service from doctors and nurses.

4 *Conventional/Professional* medicine involves the use of drugs, unlike alternative forms of medicine.

5 Several surgeons may be needed in *complex/adverse* or difficult medical operations.

6 Health systems should focus on the treatment of mental conditions, as well as *physical/conventional* healthcare.

7 Hospitals can suffer *illegal/adverse* conditions, such as underfunding or overcrowding.

8 It takes many years of *medical/professional* study to become a doctor.

9 When giving drugs to patients, it is crucially important that the quantity provided is *adequate/precise*.

CRITICAL THINKING

At the end of this unit, you will structure body paragraphs in an essay. Look at this unit's writing task in the box below.

> 'Avoiding preventable illnesses is the responsibility of individuals and their families, not governments.'
>
> Do you agree?

1 Work in groups. Look at the list of actions that people can take to avoid becoming ill. Try to agree on the five most important.

> washing your hands frequently   taking regular exercise
> getting enough fresh air   having recommended vaccinations
> cleaning your teeth   avoiding sunburn   not smoking
> reducing stress   sleeping enough   drinking enough water
> eating healthily   doing what makes you happy

2 Look at your list of the five most important actions and answer the questions below.

   1 How can individuals and families help themselves to take these actions?
   2 How can the government help people to take these actions?

3 Look at the statements below. Which statements are in favour of individual responsibility for preventative healthcare. Which are against?

   1 Healthcare is extremely expensive for governments, and medical evidence strongly suggests that lifestyle is a major indicator of health.
   2 People should be able to choose their own lifestyle.
   3 People have different situations, so they need to decide what is most beneficial for them.
   4 Many people want to eat healthily, but get tempted by advertising for junk food.
   5 Some people cannot afford to use gyms and other sports facilities.
   6 Health advice changes so frequently that people get confused about what they should and should not do.
   7 The easiest thing is to do nothing, which means many people do not take the steps needed to improve their health.
   8 Health education, not only in schools, is needed.
   9 If people do not take personal responsibility, they will lose the ability to make good choices.

WRITING

GRAMMAR FOR WRITING

Articles

Articles are essential in both spoken and written English. Knowing how to use them properly is therefore important to the accuracy of academic writing. The way that English uses articles is different from some other languages, but there are some rules you can follow.

Definite article (*the*)

a *The* is used when we refer to something specific which has been mentioned before: *the rules*.

b *The* is used for nouns when there is only one example of something: *the moon*.

c *The* is used for ordinal numbers: *the second*.

d *The* is used with superlative adjectives: *the biggest*.

Indefinite article (*a/an*)

e *A* and *an* are used to introduce single, countable nouns for the first time: *a book*.

Zero article (no article)

f No articles are needed for uncountable nouns when talking about things in general: *Water is vital for life*.

g No articles are needed for countable nouns when talking about things in general: *Doctors work hard*.

h No articles are needed for some proper nouns, like the names of most countries or people: *Ali is from Jordan*.

1 Read sentences (1–7) below. Decide which rule above (a–h) each one follows.

1 You should usually take medicine after meals. _____
2 It was the worst epidemic for many years. _____
3 It comes from India. _____
4 The British Medical Association is very well respected. _____
5 Obese children are becoming more common. _____
6 The first time you visit the doctor, you will need to register. _____
7 A doctor and a homeopath were arguing. The doctor said ... _____ and _____

2 Complete the sentences below with *a, an, the* or zero article (–).

1 When travelling, it's usually easier to carry _____ pills than _____ bottle of medicine.

2 _____ alternative medicine is popular in _____ China.

3 _____ last time I was in hospital was 2010.

4 _____ best facility in the city is _____ Royal Hospital.

5 However, _____ further research into this specific area may be necessary.

6 It can be argued that _____ homeopathy does _____ no harm as _____ additional treatment.

7 _____ cost effectiveness is _____ important issue in healthcare.

8 In addition, _____ homeopathy is _____ ancient system of _____ medicine.

EXPLANATION

Language of concession

When you present an argument in writing, you often need to mention opposing arguments. We can introduce opposing views with the language of concession. We join sentences or clauses using certain phrases which show that there is a difference of opinion.

- Homeopathy seems to be ineffective. **Other people claim that** it works.

Simple language of concession

- Homeopathy seems to be ineffective **but** people claim that it works.
- Homeopathy seems to be ineffective. **However,** people claim that it works.

More complex language of concession

- Homeopathy seems to be ineffective. **Nevertheless,** people still use it.
- **Even though / Despite the fact that / In spite of the fact that** homeopathy seems to be ineffective, people still use it.
- **Despite / In spite of** the ineffectiveness of homeopathy, people still use it.

3 Make sentences using the prompts below. You may need to add other words.

1 Conventional medicine / effective / even though / unpleasant side effects.

2 Many people argue / homeopathy should be part of / health service. However, / critics argue / denies other people / proven treatments.

3 Homeopathy / popular choice for many / in spite of the fact that / no scientific evidence / it works.

4 Ayurveda / still commonly practised in the twenty-first century / despite the fact that / nearly 3,500 years old.

5 British Medical Association / opposed to the state funding / homeopathy / but / government / still considering funding it.

6 Many people think homeopathy / not work. Nevertheless, / people should have / right to access / if they think it works.

ACADEMIC WRITING SKILLS

EXPLANATION

Writing an introduction to an essay (2)

The introduction to a piece of academic writing should include some of the features below.

a a general introduction to the topic
b the main aim or purpose of the essay
c limited background information
d an initial response to the question
e the definition of the topic
f the methods and results of research
g the organization of the essay
h an overview of the topic

1 Look at the introduction to the essay in Reading 2. Which features above (a–h) are used in sections (1–3)?

> (1) Who pays for healthcare? (2) The answer varies from country to country. While in some nations it is completely free for all residents, in others you can only see a doctor if you pay. (3) This essay will identify three main models of healthcare throughout the world, noting some advantages and disadvantages of each.

2 Make notes for an introduction to the essay question below.

> 'Avoiding preventable illnesses is the responsibility of individuals and their families, not governments.'
>
> Do you agree?

definition of the topic	
limited background information	
an initial response to the question	
the aim or purpose of the essay	

WRITING TASK

'Avoiding preventable illnesses is the responsibility of individuals and their families, not governments.' Do you agree?

1 Make notes for your essay using the plan below.

Paragraph	Information to include
Paragraph 1: Introduction	
Paragraph 2: Argument 1 supporting evidence / concession /solution	
Paragraph 3: Argument 2 supporting evidence / concession /solution	
Conclusion	

2 Write a first draft of your essay. Write 250–300 words.

3 Use the task checklist to review your essay for content and structure.

TASK CHECKLIST	✔
Does your introduction include some of the features from the Academic Writing Skills section?	
Have you given your opinion in your writing, and made it clear what your response to the question is in the introduction?	
Have you mentioned opposing ideas?	
Have you written 250–300 words?	

4 Make any necessary changes to your essay.

5 Now use the language checklist to edit your essay for language errors which are common to B2 learners.

LANGUAGE CHECKLIST	✔
Have you used articles (*the*, *a*, no article) correctly?	
Have you used the language of concession (*despite*, *although*, *however*, etc.) to show opposing views to your own arguments?	
Have you used an appropriate range of medical and academic vocabulary in your essay?	
Have you used the adjective forms of academic nouns?	

6 Make any necessary changes to your essay.

OBJECTIVES REVIEW

7 Check your objectives.

I can ...

watch and understand a
video about alternative   very   not very
medicine   well   well

skim for key words
                               very   not very
                               well   well

write an introduction to
an essay   very   not very
                               well   well

structure body
paragraphs in an essay   very   not very
                               well   well

WORDLIST

UNIT VOCABULARY		ACADEMIC VOCABULARY
cosmetic surgery (n)	remedy (n)	adequate (adj)
disease (n)	sedentary lifestyle (n)	complex (adj)
disease epidemic (n)	synthetic (adj)	conventional (adj)
illness (n)	treatment (n)	illegal (adj)
natural (adj)	underfunding (n)	medical (adj)
patent (n)		physical (adj)
preventable illness (n)		precise (adj)
		professional (adj)

LEARNING OBJECTIVES

Watch and listen	Watch and understand a video about roller coasters
Reading skills	Preview a topic before reading
Academic writing skills	Write topic sentences for body paragraphs
Writing task	Structure 'for and against' arguments in essays

UNL⌀CK YOUR KNOWLEDGE

1 Work with a partner. Decide how risky the activities below are
   (low, high or extremely high risk).

   1 rock climbing   6 working as a police officer
   2 cooking   7 travelling in a helicopter
   3 eating chocolate   8 smoking
   4 going on holiday   9 doing housework
   5 horse riding   10 motorcycle racing

2 For each activity, discuss how risk can be managed to make it safer.

3 What is the riskiest thing you have done? How did you try to
   minimize the risk?

WATCH AND LISTEN

PREPARING TO WATCH

USING YOUR
KNOWLEDGE TO
PREDICT CONTENT

1 You are going to watch a video about risk. Before you watch, discuss the questions below with a partner.

1 Why do people take risks in their lives?
2 Why do we sometimes enjoy dangerous or frightening situations?

UNDERSTANDING
KEY VOCABULARY

2 Read the sentences below. Which of the adjectives in bold are positive? Which are negative?

1 Being on a roller coaster is really **disorientating** – you don't know which way is up or which is down.
2 I couldn't cope with really **harsh** living conditions, like in the desert or the Arctic.
3 I know some people find bullfighting **thrilling**, but I get no enjoyment at all from watching it.
4 When planes do acrobatics, they make it look **uncontrolled** – but actually they know exactly what they're doing.
5 Being in an underwater cave and having no idea what you'll see next was really **exhilarating**. I can't wait to go again.

3 Match the definitions below to the adjectives in Exercise 2.

1 extremely exciting: _____ , _____
2 unpleasant and difficult: _____
3 makes you confused about what you're doing or where you're going:
_____

4 free – you can't make something do what you want it to do:
_____

WHILE WATCHING

UNDERSTANDING
MAIN IDEAS

4 ▶ Watch the video. How does it answer the two questions in Exercise 1?

5 Work in pairs. Complete the sentences below.

1 It's rather surprising that people like roller coasters because …
2 Some examples of natural risks shown in the video are …
3 Roller coasters are actually safe because …
4 Some ways people experience thrills are …
5 Roller coasters are the easiest way to get excitement safely because …

6 Look at the diagram about the chemical and physical effects of danger on humans. Complete it with words from the box.

faster   adrenalin   feel good   withstand pain   alert   stronger

Extreme circumstances

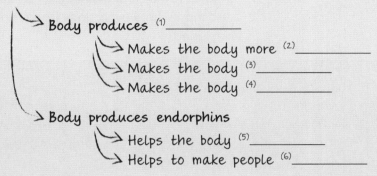

Body produces ⁽¹⁾_____
    Makes the body more ⁽²⁾_____
    Makes the body ⁽³⁾_____
    Makes the body ⁽⁴⁾_____
Body produces endorphins
    Helps the body ⁽⁵⁾_____
    Helps to make people ⁽⁶⁾_____

7 ▶ Watch the video again to check your answers to Exercises 5 and 6.

8 Work in small groups. Discuss the questions below.

1 Have you ever been on a roller coaster or other theme-park ride? If so, how did you feel? If not, would you like to go on one? Why / Why not?
2 Which of the dangerous activities mentioned in the video do you think is the most dangerous? Why?
3 Have you experienced danger? Say what happened and how you felt.

DISCUSSION

9 Work with a partner. Discuss the questions below.

1 What are the greatest risks that people face in everyday life?
2 Do you think our lives are too safe these days?
3 Is it possible to live life without risk?

READING 1

PREPARING TO READ

UNDERSTANDING KEY VOCABULARY

1 Match words and phrases (1–7) to definitions (a–g).

1 sail the seven seas
2 cut it fine
3 contingency
4 all-inclusive holiday
5 trial and error
6 play it safe
7 paragliding

a to do something just in time
b to solve a problem by making (and learning from) mistakes
c plan for possible future outcomes
d to be careful and not take risks
e a sport involving floating in the air attached to a parachute
f to travel widely and extensively
g a vacation where everything (food, drink, etc.) is included

Previewing

Before you read a text on a particular topic, it can be useful to think about your own knowledge and views on this topic. Also, ask yourself if there are any questions you hope the text will answer. This will help you develop a greater interest in the text and make it easier to understand.

2 You are going to read a quiz called 'Are you a risk-taker or are you risk-averse?' Before you read, discuss these questions with a partner.

1 In what areas of our everyday lives can we be risk-takers?
2 What kinds of question will check if you are a risk-taker?
3 Look at the words and phrases in Exercise 1. Predict how they might be used in the quiz.
4 Do you think the quiz will show you to be a risk-taker or risk-averse?

WHILE READING

3 Read the quiz and circle your response to each question.

READING FOR MAIN IDEAS

4 Work with a partner Add up how many (a), (b) or (c) answers you circled. What do you think the difference is between them?

Are you a risk-taker, or are you risk-averse?

Do our quiz to find out whether you love living on the edge of danger, or whether you would rather be safe at home!

1 What sports activities sound best to you?
   a free climbing, paragliding and horse riding
   b cycling and swimming
   c watching sport on TV

2 You've just won a lot of money. What do you do with it?
   a You buy a bright red, high-performance car. It is sure to go up in value.
   b You use the money to expand your family's successful business.
   c You put it in the bank in case you need it for an emergency later.

3 Your train leaves at 12:00. What time do you arrive at the station?
   a 11:59. There's nothing wrong with cutting it fine.
   b 10–15 minutes before it's due to leave.
   c 45 minutes ahead of schedule. This leaves plenty of time in case things go wrong.

4 What would be your dream holiday?
   a sailing the seven seas in a yacht
   b exploring a European city on a weekend break
   c going to the same all-inclusive resort you've been going to for the last ten years

5 Do you read the instructions before you use a new piece of equipment?
   a You never read them – you prefer learning by trial and error.
   b You only look at them if you get stuck.
   c You always read them from cover to cover before you unpack the item.

6 You're eating out at a restaurant. What do you order?
   a You ask the waiter to surprise you.
   b You ask for advice and look at what other diners have ordered.
   c You play it safe and go with what you know.

7 Which of these jobs appeals to you most?
   a an astronaut
   b a pilot
   c an airline check-in clerk

5 Complete the explanation of the scores with the correct letters from the quiz.

1 If you answered mainly _____ , you are happy to take risks, but only if you're sure things will turn out all right.

2 If you answered mainly _____ , you prefer a comfortable life, where things are predictable and there are few surprises. Don't be afraid to take a chance every now and then!

3 If you answered mainly _____ , you like to live life on the edge. You never know what's around the corner. Just be careful you don't take one risk too many!

READING FOR DETAIL

6 Read the quiz again. Match formal phrases (1–7) to answers in the quiz.

1 making a high-risk motoring purchase   _2a_
2 a nautical adventure   _____
3 allowing contingency time   _____
4 a risk-free pastime   _____
5 considering recommendations and observation findings   _____
6 experimentation
7 space exploration   _____

READING BETWEEN THE LINES

7 Answer the questions below. Use the information in the quiz to help you.

1 Can watching sport on TV ever be dangerous?
2 What are the advantages of investing your money in a family business?
3 What is the problem with always cutting it fine?
4 Why do more people not 'sail the seven seas' when they go on holiday?
5 Why might it be a bad idea to read the instructions from cover to cover?
6 What could happen if you asked a waiter to surprise you?
7 Why might the job of an airline check-in clerk appeal to some people?

DISCUSSION

8 Work with a partner. Discuss the questions below.

1 Compare your quiz results with a partner. How much of a risk-taker are you?
2 Do you think tests like this are useful? Why? / Why not?

READING 2

PREPARING TO READ

USING YOUR
KNOWLEDGE TO
PREDICT CONTENT

1 Work with a partner. Answer the questions about your country or other countries you know.

1 Do you have to wear a seatbelt when driving, or a helmet when riding a motorbike?
2 Is unhealthy food or drink prohibited, or is it taxed heavily?
3 Does the government warn against risky activities in posters or TV commercials? Which ones?

UNDERSTANDING
KEY VOCABULARY

2 Complete definitions (1–7) with words from the box.

> compulsory   prudence   regulations   infringe
> responsibility   legislation   prohibiting

1 If something is _____ , it means that you have no choice whether to do it or not.
2 To _____ on someone's freedom is to take it away or limit it.
3 _____ means not taking any unnecessary risks.
4 _____ is a formal word for the making of laws.
5 By _____ something you are effectively making it illegal.
6 If you are liable for something, it means you have legal _____ for it.
7 _____ are sets of rules established by an organization.

3 Which of the issues below do you think governments should control?

1 national security
2 road safety
3 financial support for people in poverty
4 disease prevention
5 safety at work
6 online security
7 protection from injury in the home
8 provision of healthcare
9 smoking
10 news services

A government has a duty to protect its citizens from personal, professional and financial risk.

Give reasons for and against the statement and state your opinion.

Governments of some countries see it as their responsibility to control the amount and kind of risk that their citizens are exposed to. They can use legislation to protect personal health, prevent injury in the workplace and help people handle financial matters. In other nations, citizens are expected to take care of themselves and carry the responsibility of their own safety and that of others. This essay will explore the advantages and disadvantages of both approaches.

In the UK, the government protects its population from risk in a number of areas. It makes it compulsory to wear a seatbelt or helmet while on the roads, and manages risk of disease by taxing or prohibiting unhealthy foods or cigarettes. It prevents the spread of disease by investing in vaccination programmes and health education. Workers are protected from harm through government-implemented health and safety regulations and companies and managers are liable for employee death or injury. This has resulted in 800 fewer deaths per year in the British workplace. In terms of financial protection, the UK government gives those in poverty access to healthcare, food and shelter. It also tries to prevent fraud and other financial crime, while encouraging economic prudence through methods such as saving.

While some people believe the UK government acts in the best interests of their citizens, others feel it infringes on the freedom of the public. They object to paying hefty financial penalties (for example, for riding a motorbike without a helmet), even though they may personally accept the risk. People who smoke and eat unhealthy food argue that they are posing less risk to their health than horse riders or skiers and it is dangerous sports which should be banned, not food. Businesses complain that health and safety regulations mean that they spend too much time and money protecting against very low risks, and that this has a negative impact on their business and the national economy. Others reject government advice about saving money as hypocritical when they notice an increase in state borrowing.

In conclusion, we can see that there are both benefits and risks attached to a government that tries to control the safety of its citizens. This can reduce accidents, disease and crime, and cater for the basic needs of all members of society. Conversely, however, over-protective legislation can limit individual freedom and cause resentment. It can also suggest that people do not have to be responsible for their own actions. In my opinion, a country with tight controls provides a pleasant and safe environment. However, legislation needs to be carefully monitored to ensure it is appropriate, up-to-date and not excessively restrictive.

WHILE READING

4 Read the essay. Which of the issues in Exercise 3 does it mention?

5 Find the following words in the text. Then look for a synonym for each of these words in the text.

1 countries   3 people   5 regulations
2 injury   4 financial   6 liable

READING BETWEEN THE LINES

6 Work with a partner. Discuss the questions below.

1 What is the danger if managers are not liable for accidents in the workplace?
2 What does the writer mean by *hefty financial penalties*?
3 What sort of health and safety legislation do you think businesses complain about?
4 Do you think the writer is a risk-taker?

DISCUSSION

7 Work with a partner. Discuss the questions below.

1 Do you agree with people who say that dangerous sports should be banned? If so, which ones?
2 Should people take responsibility for their own risks?
3 What new legislation should be implemented to further protect people from risk in society?

⊙ LANGUAGE DEVELOPMENT

LANGUAGE OF FREEDOM

1 Complete the table with the words from the box.

allow   ban   curb   limit   criminalize   permit   restrict   legalize
grant   authorize

promoting freedom	restricting freedom

2 Choose the best word (a, b or c) to complete the sentences.

1 Certain countries completely _____ the sale of guns.
   a restrict   **b** ban   **c** grant

2 The president will _____ the building of several new colleges.
   a authorize   **b** criminalize   **c** legalize

3 Governments _____ the sale of harmful drugs to make them illegal.
   a allow   **b** criminalize   **c** curb

4 There will be a _____ on the sale of cigarettes at the end of the month – you will only be able to buy them if you are over 18.
   a limit   **b** ban   **c** legalize

5 If countries _____ people the right to vote, they should use their vote carefully.
   a grant   **b** limit   **c** authorize

EXPLANATION

Academic nouns

There are many formal academic nouns which can improve your essay writing. A lot of these end in -*tion* and -*sion*. Using these words instead of shorter, more common nouns is a feature of academic writing.

3 Replace the nouns in bold in sentences (1–7) with the words from the box.

> regulations   legislation   prevention   objection   reduction
> confusion   dissatisfaction

1 The **fall** in numbers shows that many people think the risks are too high.
2 The government intends to introduce new **laws** to control migration.
3 Workplaces must introduce more strategies with regard to the **stopping** of risk.
4 There is a considerable amount of **unhappiness** about recent changes to financial policy.
5 The company has brought in extra safety **rules** to prevent further accidents.
6 There was **chaos** when the decision was announced.
7 Companies have outlined a key **complaint** to the recent change in government policy.

CRITICAL THINKING

At the end of this unit, you will write a 'for and against' essay. Look at a similar writing task in the box below.

> 'Taking greater risks leads to larger personal, professional and financial rewards.'
>
> Discuss the arguments for and against this statement and give your opinion.

EVALUATE

1 In this essay question, the risks have been divided into three topics: everyday life, work life, and your finances. Read risks (1–12) below and decide whether they are personal, professional or financial. They may belong to more than one topic.

1 investing in get-rich-quick schemes _financial_
2 not wearing protective equipment _____
3 not reading instructions _____
4 avoiding paying tax _____
5 ignoring or breaking the law _____
6 not doing a risk assessment in your office _____
7 regularly being late for work _____
8 spending money freely _____
9 not taking out house insurance _____
10 arriving with seconds to spare _____
11 spending on credit _____
12 not wearing a seatbelt _____

APPLY

2 Match risks (1–12) to rewards (a–l) below.

a maximizes profit _1 (investing in get-rich-quick schemes)_
b means that you can get in and out of a car more easily _____
c you can sleep for longer _____
d you are more comfortable _____
e you don't have to waste time waiting at the station or airport _____
f you save money on the insurance policy _____
g you learn more effectively by working it out for yourself _____
h you do not have to pay money now, but at a later time _____
i you can buy things you really like and have a good time _____
j you keep money for yourself rather than giving it to the government _____
k some things you really enjoy doing may be illegal _____
l you can use the time more effectively on other parts of your job _____

3 Work with a partner. What are the arguments against taking each risk in Exercise 2?

WRITING

GRAMMAR FOR WRITING

Cause and effect

There are simple verb phrases we can use to show the cause and effect of certain actions.

- Taking risks **results in** greater rewards.
- Taking risks **leads to** greater rewards.
- Taking risks **means** greater rewards.

Notice how we can also use more complex linkers to show the connection between two sentences.

- Maximizing profit is encouraged in investment banking. **As a result of this**, some bankers take on too much risk in their portfolio.
- Maximizing profit is encouraged in investment banking. **Because of this**, some bankers take on too much risk in their portfolio.
- Maximizing profit is encouraged in investment banking. **Consequently**, some bankers take on too much risk in their portfolio.

1 Complete each sentence (b) with a verb phrase so that it means the same as sentence (a).

1 a If you take fewer risks, you receive smaller rewards.
   b Taking fewer risks _____

2 a If you manage risk carefully, everybody stays safer.
   b Managing risk carefully _____

3 a If there is excessive risk-taking, chaos may follow.
   b Excessive risk-taking _____

2 Complete the sentences below with your own ideas.

1 Some people avoid paying tax to save money. Consequently, _____
_____

2 Many groups have criticized banks' excessive risk-taking. As a result of this, _____

3 It is very difficult to predict how long the bus will take to get to the station. Because of this, _____

Conditional language

EXPLANATION

We can use *if*-clauses to add a condition to an opinion.

Governments should legislate against extremely hazardous activities
if they do not attempt to control too much of our personal lives.

In formal writing, we can use more complex linkers to replace *if*. It is also possible
to reverse the order of the clauses.

- **Provided that** they do not attempt to control too much of our
  personal lives, governments should legislate against extremely
  hazardous activities.
- Governments should legislate against extremely hazardous activities
  provided that they do not attempt to control too much of our
  personal lives.
- **As long as** they do not attempt to control too much of our personal
  lives, governments should legislate against extremely hazardous
  activities.
- Governments should legislate against extremely hazardous activities
  as long as they do not attempt to control too much of our personal
  lives.
- **On condition that** they do not attempt to control too much of
  our personal lives, governments should legislate against extremely
  hazardous activities.
- Governments should legislate against extremely hazardous activities
  on condition that they do not attempt to control too much of our
  lives.

3 Work in pairs. Complete the sentences below with a suitable linker and
condition.

1 Individuals should be allowed to do whatever they like _____

2 Risk is acceptable in the workplace _____

3 Potential problems connected to risk-taking can be minimized _____

4 Financial investments do not need to be risky _____

ACADEMIC WRITING SKILLS

Topic sentences in body paragraphs

The *topic sentence* of a paragraph is generally its first sentence. Here are four examples.

- Governments of some countries see it as their responsibility to control the amount and kind of risk that their citizens are exposed to.
- In the UK, the government protects its population from risk in a number of areas.
- While some people believe the UK government acts in the best interests of their citizens, others feel it infringes on the freedom of the public.
- In conclusion, we can see that there are both benefits and risks attached to a government that tries to control the safety of its citizens.

1 Circle the correct words.

  1 A topic sentence should identify the *main idea/detail* in the paragraph.
  2 The focus of a topic sentence should be *specific/general*.
  3 A topic sentence generally provides *no/many* examples to back up its main point.

2 Work with a partner. Read the topic sentences below and decide which sentence (a or b) would be the most appropriate to use in an essay.

  1 a There are different definitions of risk-taking and success.
    b One of the definitions of success is 'the favourable outcome of something attempted', another is 'the attainment of wealth, fame, etc.'
  2 a If the only questions asked are those which we can already answer, then there can be no unexpected positive results.
    b Positive results are impossible.
  3 a 51% of people believe that risk-taking is bad.
    b On the other hand, in the case of dangerous risks, the consequences are more likely to be negative.
  4 a In conclusion, the answer to this question is dependent on the level of risk involved.
    b There are three further points which need to be discussed.

WRITING TASK

'If children are never exposed to risk, they will never be able to cope with risk.'

Give reasons for and against this statement and give your opinion.

PLAN AND WRITE
A FIRST DRAFT

1 Look again at the essay on page 76. Consider the arguments for and against the essay title above. Use the paragraph structure below.

- Paragraph 1: Introduction
- Paragraph 2: Arguments for
- Paragraph 3: Arguments against
- Paragraph 4: Conclusion

2 Make notes on your essay below.

Paragraph 2: Arguments that children need to be exposed to some risk

Evidence 1: _____

_____

_____

Evidence 2: _____

_____

_____

Evidence 3: _____

_____

_____

Paragraph 3: Arguments that children should be protected from all risk

Evidence 1: _____

_____

_____

Evidence 2: _____

_____

_____

Evidence 3: _____

_____

3 Look again at your notes for Paragraphs 2 and 3 and decide what your overall opinion is. Do you think that children should be exposed to risk? Write a one-sentence response to this question, providing evidence.

4 Write a first draft of your essay. Write 250–300 words.

5 Use the task checklist to review your essay for content and structure.

TASK CHECKLIST	✔
Have you given each body paragraph a suitable opening topic sentence?	
Have you used the correct essay structure in your writing?	
Is the evidence you have used appropriate and well-chosen?	
Have you written 250–300 words?	

6 Make any necessary changes to your essay.

7 Use the language checklist to edit your essay for language errors which are common to B2 learners.

LANGUAGE CHECKLIST	✔
Have you used a good range of topic-related vocabulary?	
Have you used cause and effect language correctly?	
Have you used conditional language correctly?	

8 Make any necessary changes to your essay.

OBJECTIVES REVIEW

9 Check your objectives.

I can ...

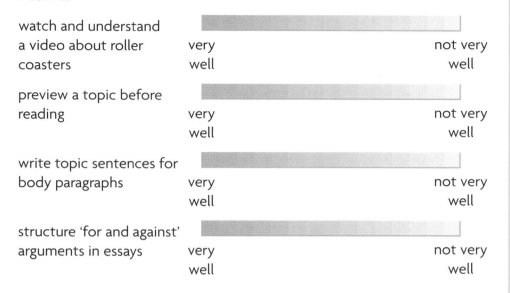

	very well	not very well
watch and understand a video about roller coasters		
preview a topic before reading		
write topic sentences for body paragraphs		
structure 'for and against' arguments in essays		

WORDLIST

UNIT VOCABULARY			ACADEMIC VOCABULARY
all-inclusive (adj)	grant (v)	portfolio (n)	confusion (n)
allow (v)	great (adj)	prohibit (v)	dissatisfaction (n)
authorize (v)	harsh (adj)	prudence (n)	legislation (n)
ban (v)	infringe on (v)	regulation (n)	objection (n)
compulsory (adj)	legalize (v)	responsibility (n)	prevention (n)
contingency (n)	liable (adj)	restrict (v)	reduction (n)
criminalize (v)	limit (v)	thrilling (adj)	regulation (n)
cut it fine (ph)	paragliding (n)	uncomfortable (adj)	
disorientating (adj)	permit (v)	uncontrolled (adj)	
exhilarating (adj)	play safe (ph)		

LEARNING OBJECTIVES

Watch and listen	Watch and understand a video about making chocolate
Reading skills	Activate prior knowledge
Academic writing skills	Add detail to your writing
Writing task	Write a description of a process

UNLOCK YOUR KNOWLEDGE

1 Work with a partner. Use the words in the box to describe the processes below.

first   then   after that   next   later   finally

1 making a cup of coffee
   First you have to fill the kettle with water. Then you heat the water so that it boils. After that, you need to ...
2 travelling to your English class from home
3 writing an essay
4 making your favourite dish
5 getting a new job

2 Why is it important to know how to describe processes in academic writing?

WATCH AND LISTEN

PREPARING TO WATCH

USING YOUR
KNOWLEDGE TO
PREDICT CONTENT

1 Work with a partner. You are going to watch a video about how chocolate is made. Before you watch, answer the questions below.

1 Where does chocolate come from?
2 How do you think chocolate is made?
3 Is chocolate a natural product or are there many artificial additives?

UNDERSTANDING
KEY VOCABULARY

2 Match verbs (a–h) to definitions (1–8).

a harvest	1 remove the outer part of a nut or bean
b melt	2 make something into a powder or small pieces
c dry	3 put something in boxes or containers to be sold
d roast	4 pick and collect crops
e mould	5 heat something so it turns to liquid
f package	6 cook in an oven
g shell	7 shape, form or design something
h grind	8 remove excess water from something

3 Verbs (a–h) in Exercise 2 relate to different stages in the chocolate-making process. Predict the correct order.

4 Watch the video to check your answers.

WHILE WATCHING

5 ▶ Watch again. Complete the flow chart below about the chocolate-making process.

(1) __Beans__ are harvested

Fermented and dried (at least a (2)_____).

(3)_____ in sacks

and (4)_____ .

Beans are (5)_____ to leave nibs.

Cocoa (6)_____ is added.

Milk and (7)_____ are mixed in with the chocolate.

(8)_____ powder is mixed with chocolate and heated.

(9)_____ , cooled and reheated.

Packaged, sold and (10)_____ .

6 Match stages (1–7) to reasons (a–g).

The chocolate-manufacturing process

1 beans are split
2 beans are fermented
3 beans are roasted at the correct temperature
4 beans go through a grinder
5 cocoa butter is mixed in
6 tempering the chocolate
7 the mixture is moulded

a otherwise the taste is affected
b results in large pieces
c to make individual chocolates
d so the insides can be checked
e to make them into a liquid
f to remove their bitterness
g to make the chocolate smooth

7 Work with a partner. Discuss the questions below and choose the correct answers.

1 What weather conditions in Ghana, Ivory Coast, Brazil and Indonesia do you think make them suitable for growing cocoa?
   a wet and warm   b cold and windy   c warm and dry
2 Which other countries do you think produce a lot of cocoa?
   a Ecuador and Cameroon
   b Canada and Spain
   c Kenya and India
3 At which stage of the chocolate-making process do you think the most profit is made?
   a growing   b manufacturing   c selling

DISCUSSION

8 Work with a partner. Discuss the questions below.

1 Is chocolate popular in your country? Why / Why not?
2 Why are chocolate companies criticized for advertising to children?
3 Cocoa-bean farmers are not paid much for their beans, but the price of chocolate is high. Why is this?
4 Do you think this situation should change? If so, how?

READING 1

PREPARING TO READ

Before you read a text, it helps to think of what you already know about its subject. This will help you understand a difficult text because you will know what information to expect. It is also useful to think of some questions that you hope the text will answer. This will help you to focus on the important information. When you have read the text, you can make notes about what you have learnt. By approaching reading in this way, you can find out what you want or need to know about the subject.

ACTIVATING PRIOR KNOWLEDGE

1 Work with a partner. Your teacher has asked you to give a short presentation about the history of silk.

1 Before you research the topic, write notes in the first column of the table below.
2 What do you need to know to make a good presentation? Write questions in the second column.

The history of silk		
what I know about silk	what I want to know	what I learnt

2 Read the article. Check to see whether your facts are mentioned.
Write any answers to your questions in the third column of the table.

A BRIEF HISTORY OF SILK

Comfortable to wear no matter if the weather is hot or cold, silk is as popular today as it was 5,000 years ago when it was first manufactured. However, the history of silk has not always been as smooth as the fabric itself.

Today's basic silk-production process has changed very little since it first began. The fabric comes from silkworms which, although tiny when born, grow rapidly in size. Indeed, on a strict diet of mulberry leaves, it is estimated that they increase in weight by 10,000% over the first six weeks of their life. When they are fully grown, the silkworms create a cocoon – a protective shell made of silk. They then crawl inside in order to prepare for their next stage of development. However, for commercial silk production, these cocoons are then boiled, killing the worm inside, to ensure that the silk is not damaged. After this, the silk is gathered and prepared. A single cocoon can produce between 300 and 900 metres of silk thread.

Although today silk is both grown and worn worldwide, the original production of silk was restricted to China. Indeed, it was so important that at one time it was only the emperor and his close family who were allowed to wear it. The Chinese were initially very protective of the silk-manufacturing process. To smuggle either the silkworms or mulberry leaves out of China was punishable by death. Despite the risks, a princess in the fifth century concealed some silkworm eggs in her hair and took them to her fiancé's Asian kingdom. Likewise, in the sixth century, two monks managed to take some eggs all the way back to their native Byzantium (modern-day Istanbul, in Turkey). This was an event of great importance, since Europe was from that point able to manufacture its own silk.

Prior to the monks' success in bringing the silkworms out of China, Europeans were dependent on merchants bringing the fabric from East Asia across the mountain roads of Central Asia and the Middle East. Indeed, so much silk was transported that this trade route became known as the Silk Road. By the time of the Roman Empire, silk had become popular around the Mediterranean, although it was very expensive.

China is still the world's main producer of silk, manufacturing around 80% of global supply. India is the second-largest producer, with around 15%. Although man-made fibres are cheaper and easier to manufacture, the beauty of silk is difficult to match, and there is always likely to be a large international market.

Silkworm cocoons

WHILE READING

3 Read the article again. Are the statements below true (T), false (F) or the article does not say (DNS)?

1 Silk is suitable for different climates. _____
2 Silkworms are usually killed in order to make silk. _____
3 Silkworms can grow to 5 cm long. _____
4 Silkworms have a varied diet. _____
5 Thousands of people were put to death for smuggling silkworms out of China. _____
6 Silk is less popular today than it was before. _____
7 The Silk Road passed through the important city of Petra in Jordan. _____
8 World silk production is dominated by two countries. _____

4 Complete sentences (1–5) with the correct ending (a–d).

1 Before silk is gathered, silkworm cocoons are ...
   a put in the freezer.
   b opened.
   c checked for quality.
   d put in hot water.
2 Historically, in China silk was worn ...
   a only by the royal family.
   b by anybody who wanted to.
   c only by the emperor.
   d only by silk farmers.
3 Silkworm eggs were smuggled back to Europe by ...
   a the Chinese.
   b merchants.
   c a princess and two monks.
   d two monks.
4 The author suggests that the Silk Road ...
   a was easy to travel on.
   b mainly carried goods from Europe.
   c was used by traders.
   d was busiest after the eggs had been smuggled out.
5 Silk is ...
   a one of the easiest fabrics to make.
   b no longer a popular material.
   c cheaper to produce than man-made fibres.
   d not only made in China.

READING BETWEEN THE LINES

MAKING INFERENCES
FROM THE TEXT

5 Complete the sentences below with your own ideas.

1 The writer says the history of silk has not been 'smooth' because …
2 The Chinese were probably 'very protective of the silk-manufacturing process' because …
3 Although it was expensive, silk had probably 'become popular around the Mediterranean' because …
4 'Man-made fibres are cheaper and easier to manufacture' because …

DISCUSSION

6 Work with a partner. Discuss the questions below.

1 Which is better for clothing: intensively farmed silk or artificial fabrics? Why?
2 Should we protect traditional industries such as silk-making, even if they are unprofitable?
3 Silk production used to be controlled by China. Do you know any similar types of trade monopolies in the modern world?

READING 2

PREPARING TO READ

USING YOUR
KNOWLEDGE TO
PREDICT CONTENT

1 Work with a partner. What do you know about how paper is made? Add as much information as you can to the ideas map.

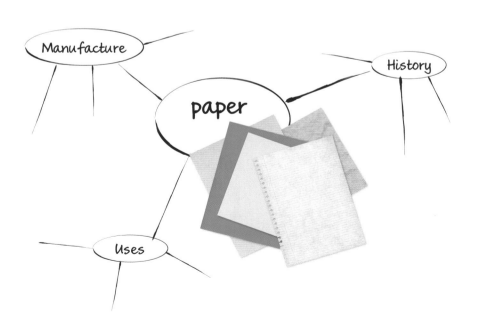

How is paper manufactured?

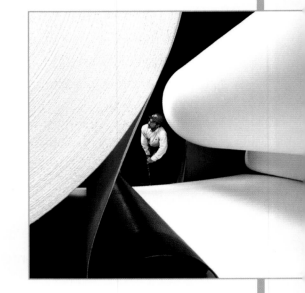

A _____

Trees are the starting point of the paper-manufacturing process. It is important that the right type of tree is used, otherwise the finished paper may not be suitable for use. Generally speaking, hardwood trees, such as oak, have short fibres, meaning that the paper made from them is weaker. However, the surface tends to be smoother and is therefore better to print on. Softwood trees, like pine, make stronger paper, but are not so good for writing on. This paper is more suited to industrial use.

B _____

Once the trees have been taken to the factory, the paper-manufacturing process begins. After the removal of the trees' outer skin, known as 'bark', the wood is passed through a chipper, which cuts it into smaller pieces of roughly the same size. Following this, the chips may be put into a digester, depending on whether a chemical called lignin is going to be removed. When lignin reacts with air and sunlight, it turns yellow, thus permanently changing the paper's colour. While this is not much of a problem for cheaper, non-permanent types of paper (such as newspaper), it needs to be removed for fine, white paper. Next, the wood pulp is cleaned and bleached by the washer before going through a beater. This machine further refines the fibres and may cut them to a certain length. Screens then remove oversized particles from the pulp, ensuring that it can pass through the next machine (called a head box) easily.

C _____

Once the pulp enters the paper machine, which is a moving conveyor belt made of fabric, it passes through four specific sections. Firstly, it goes through the former, where the pulp is turned into a continuous piece of material. Secondly, in the press section, the pulp is squeezed through large rollers under high pressure, with the intention of extracting as much water as possible. Next, the dryers remove even more water before the last section, where heavy rollers, known as calenders, smooth the paper.

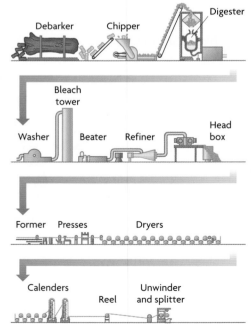

D _____

The final stage of the process prepares the paper for further use. A reel collects the paper into a user-friendly roll, which may then either be sold directly or cut into smaller-sized rolls.

WHILE READING

2 Read the first sentence of each paragraph in the article. Match headings (1–4) to paragraphs (A–D).

1 Making the product ready for market
2 Processing the raw material
3 Obtaining the raw material
4 Turning the raw material into a product

3 You are going to summarize how paper is made. Read the article again. Make notes under the four headings in Exercise 2.

4 Work with a partner. Using your notes and the diagram in the article, summarize how paper is made.

READING BETWEEN THE LINES

5 Work with a partner. What do these phrases from the text mean?

1 starting point
2 generally speaking
3 more suited to
4 further refines
5 with the intention of

DISCUSSION

6 Work with a partner. Discuss the questions below.

1 Do you prefer to read on paper or on electronic devices? Why?
2 What effect do you think the internet has had on the paper industry?
3 Do you think we will ever stop using paper? Why? / Why not?

⊙ LANGUAGE DEVELOPMENT

Academic verb synonyms

When describing a process, we need to use a range of verbs. If you repeat the same verbs too often, the text becomes repetitive. You can avoid this by learning synonyms of common academic verbs. Try to use them in your writing.

1 Match verbs (1–10) to their academic synonyms (a–j).

1 build
2 change
3 give out
4 grow
5 show
6 do
7 talk to
8 remove
9 improve
10 appear

a alter
b assemble
c enhance
d emerge
e distribute
f cultivate
g display
h consult with
i extract
j undertake

2 Complete the sentences below with words (a–j) from Exercise 1.

1 Robots are used to _____ the component parts and glue them together.
2 The silkworms _____ from their eggs after a few weeks.
3 Tempering does not _____ the taste of the chocolate.
4 By adding orange or mint, you can _____ the flavour of chocolate, making it less bitter.
5 Large farms are required in order to _____ cocoa plants commercially.
6 When chocolate reaches the shops, it is necessary to _____ it attractively on the shelves so that more people buy it.
7 When starting a new business, it is wise to _____ other experts in the field.
8 Before you _____ any project, it is important to plan it properly.
9 Once the product has been manufactured, it is necessary to _____ it to shops in order to sell it.
10 This process will _____ waste products.

Nominalization

Another way to avoid repetition when describing a process is to replace some verb phrases with noun phrases. This is called nominalization. We can change a verb or verb phrase into a noun by adding a noun suffix, such as *-ion*, *-ment* or *-ness*: *pay – payment, be fair – fairness, employ – employment*.

- The first step is for farmers to **cultivate the crops**. (verb + noun)
- **Crop cultivation** is the first step.

Or sometimes we use a gerund, (*-ing* form).

- In the first stage, people **strip the bark**. (verb + noun)
- The first stage is **bark stripping**.

Sometimes we need to use a preposition in the noun phrase.

- It is very expensive for producers to **transport chocolate**. (verb + noun)
- **Transportation of chocolate** is very expensive. (noun + preposition + noun)

Sometimes a verb has a different noun form.

- If the **temperature rises**, the **silkworms may die** before they complete their cocoons. (noun + verb, noun + verb)
- A **temperature rise** can cause the **death of the silkworms** before they complete their cocoons.

Notice that the word order often changes. Remember every sentence must still include a verb.

3 Nominalize the verb phrases in these sentences to make noun phrases.

1 After this stage, we roll the paper.
_____ occurs after this stage.

2 The last stage is when we distribute the chocolate.
_____ is the last stage.

3 Silk is created in the cocoons themselves.
_____ happens in the cocoons.

4 Chocolate takes a long time to produce.
Chocolate _____ takes a long time.

5 It is usually expensive to manufacture silk clothing.
_____ silk clothing is usually expensive.

6 Developed countries consume more chocolate.
_____ is higher in developed countries.

CRITICAL THINKING

At the end of this unit, you will write a description of a process. Look at this unit's writing task in the box below.

> Write a description of a process with which you are familiar.

UNDERSTAND

1 Match the stages in the silk-manufacturing process (1–10) to the pictures (a–j).

1 Silkworms spin their cocoons.
2 Moth lays eggs.
3 Filaments are spun and turned into thread.
4 Cocoons are boiled and softened.
5 Silk fabric is made into clothing.
6 Silkworms eat mulberry leaves.
7 Silk fabric is dyed different colours.
8 Silk thread is woven into fabric.
9 Thread is packaged and distributed.
10 Cocoons are sorted into different types.

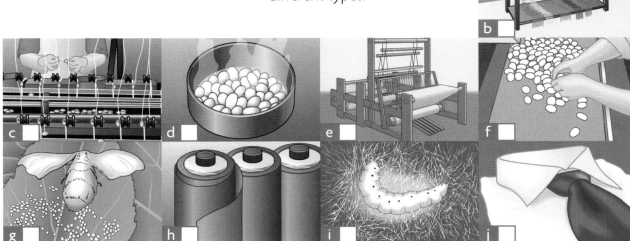

2 Write stages (a–j) from Exercise 1 in the order in which they happen in the silk-manufacturing process.

1 _____   3 _____   5 _____   7 _____   9 _____

2 _____   4 _____   6 _____   8 _____   10 _____

WRITING

GRAMMAR FOR WRITING

The passive

Passive structures are very common in describing a process, because we often do not need to say *who* carries out an action, only that it happens. We use passive structures when an agent (the person or thing that does something) is not important, is unknown or obvious.

To make a passive structure, we use the correct form of *be* followed by the past participle of the verb.

Word order is different in a passive sentence. The object of an active sentence would be the subject of a passive one.

Active: People grow silk and people wear silk worldwide.
Passive: Silk **is** both **grown** and **worn** worldwide.
(We do not need to know who grew the silk or who wears it, so the passive structure is more appropriate.)

We can also use a passive sentence when we *do* want to say who or what the agent is. This gives more importance to the object than the agent. We use *by* before the agent, and this is usually at the end of the sentence.

The chocolate **is tested** by quality controllers.
(The information we are focusing on is that the chocolate is tested.)

1 Change each sentence below so that it uses a passive structure.

   1 Paper makers make newspaper from hardwood trees.
     Newspaper _____

   2 People make the fabric into clothing.
     The fabric _____

   3 People eat chocolate at many religious festivals.
     Chocolate _____

   4 Many people consider silk to be the most luxurious fabric in the world.
     Silk _____

   5 You need patience in the silk-manufacturing process.
     Patience _____

   6 People have produced silk in China for hundreds of years.
     Silk _____

   7 People will then sell the clothes for export.
     The clothes _____

2 Correct the mistakes in the sentences below.

   1 Chocolate is make from cocoa beans.
   2 Moths are laid eggs.
   3 The grain it is made into flour in a mill.
   4 The products be are sold in the shops.
   5 After the paper is cutted, we store it in large rolls.
   6 Once this stage is finished, the silk sells.
   7 Before the process finished, the chocolate is packaged.
   8 Silkworms are eaten mulberry leaves.

Sequencing

We can add time clauses with *after*, *once*, *when*, *as soon as* and *before* to show a sequence of events.

When we begin a sentence with *after*, *once*, *when* or *as soon as*, the actions which follow are in order.

> **After** the thread is packaged, it is distributed.
> (the first action is *packaged*, the second is *distributed*)

However, if we begin a sentence with *before*, the second action is mentioned earlier.

> **Before** the thread is distributed, it is packaged.
> (the first action is *packaged*, the second is *distributed*)

We can also use the present perfect with *after*, *once*, *when* and *as soon as* to make it clear that the actions happen in a particular order.

> **Once** the thread **has been packaged**, it is distributed.

3 Link the clauses using the word in brackets. Change one (or more) of the verbs to the passive where necessary.

1 We boil the cocoons. Then we soften the cocoons. (after)
   <u>After the cocoons have been boiled, they are softened.</u>

2 The silkworms finish making their cocoons. The silkworms crawl inside. (as soon as) _____

3 The paper is cut into smaller-sized rolls. A reel collects the paper. (before) _____

4 The sun dries the beans. Various vehicles transport the beans to chocolate producers around the world. (once) _____

5 People smuggled silkworm eggs out of China. Only the Chinese could make silk. (before) _____

6 The machine cuts the fibres to length. The machine removes oversized particles. (after) _____

ACADEMIC WRITING SKILLS

Adding detail to your writing

When we write about a process, we often need to give detailed information. As well as describing what happens, we may need to explain how, why, where or when it happens. At B2 level, you will be expected to write about processes in enough detail for a reader to be able to fully understand.

(A2 level) We boil the cocoons. Then we soften the cocoons.
(B1 level) The cocoons are boiled and softened.
(B2 level) After the cocoons have been boiled in water, they are softened to release the filaments.

1 Work with a partner. What can you remember from this unit? Complete the sentences below in more detail.

1 Chocolate is made from cocoa beans
   <u>which are grown in tropical countries.</u>
2 The beans are dried in the sun _____
3 Sugar is added to the chocolate _____
4 Silk was invented by the Chinese _____
5 A princess smuggled eggs out of China _____
6 The cocoons are boiled _____
7 In the factory, the wood is cut _____
8 The paper is collected onto a user-friendly roll _____

2 Read the sentences below describing the silk-making process. Put them in the correct order.

    a The silkworms wrap the cocoon around themselves.   _____

    b The eggs hatch.   _____

    c We give the silkworms mulberry leaves.   _____

    d The moths lay eggs.   _____

    e The silkworms make a cocoon.   _____

3 Link the sentences in Exercise 2 together to form a paragraph. Use passive structures and time clauses from the Grammar for Writing section.

WRITING TASK

Write a description of a process with which you are familiar.

1 Make notes in the table below.

PLAN AND WRITE
A FIRST DRAFT

Paragraph 1: introduction to the process you are going to describe	
Paragraph 2: describe one aspect of the process (e.g. obtaining the raw material or preparing equipment)	
Paragraph 3: describe another aspect of the process (e.g. processing the raw material or creating the final product)	
Paragraph 4: describe the final part of the process (e.g. making a product ready for the end user)	

2 Write your description. Write 250–300 words.

3 Use the task checklist to review your description for content and structure.

TASK CHECKLIST	✔
Have you used an appropriate structure for this piece of writing?	
Have you clearly indicated the different stages in the process?	
Have you used the passive voice where appropriate?	
Have you made clear links between each of the stages, using sequencing language?	
Have you written 250–300 words?	

4 Make any necessary changes to your description.

5 Now use the language checklist to edit your description for language errors which are common to B2 learners.

LANGUAGE CHECKLIST	✔
Have you used academic verbs to avoid repetition where possible?	
Have you nominalized verb phrases to make noun phrases where necessary?	
Have you used a range of time phrases for sequencing?	
Have you spelt any relevant subject-specific language correctly?	

6 Make any necessary changes to your description.

OBJECTIVES REVIEW

7 Check your objectives.

I can …

watch and understand a video about making chocolate

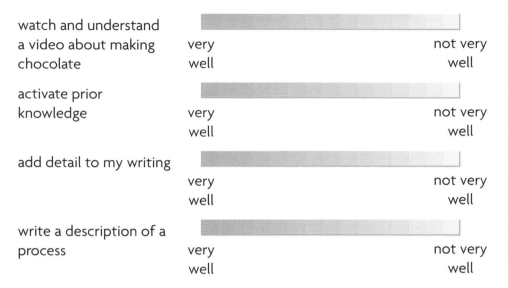

| very well | not very well |

activate prior knowledge

| very well | not very well |

add detail to my writing

| very well | not very well |

write a description of a process

| very well | not very well |

WORDLIST

UNIT VOCABULARY	ACADEMIC VOCABULARY
dry (v)	alter (v)
ferment (v)	consult (v)
grind (v)	cultivate (v)
harvest (v)	display (v)
melt (v)	distribute (v)
mould (v)	emerge (v)
package (v)	enhance (v)
roast (v)	extract (v)
shell (v)	product (n)
temper (v)	undertake (v)

LEARNING OBJECTIVES

Watch and listen	Watch and understand a video about the Three Gorges Dam
Reading skills	Identify cohesive devices (pronouns and synonyms)
Academic writing skills	Structure paragraphs
Writing task	Write a report referring to a case study

ENVIRONMENT   UNIT 6

UNL⌀CK YOUR KNOWLEDGE

Work with a partner. Discuss the questions below.

1 Why do floods and droughts occur? What impact can they have on a country?
2 What other natural disasters do you know about? What impact do they have on people and places?

WATCH AND LISTEN

PREPARING TO WATCH

USING YOUR KNOWLEDGE TO PREDICT CONTENT

1 You are going to watch a video about the building of a dam in China. Before you watch, answer the questions.

   1 Are there any major dams in your country or another country you know well? If so, why were they built?

   2 What are the benefits of dams?

   3 Are there any disadvantages to building them?

2 Work with a partner. Look at the photos from the video. Discuss what you think each one shows. What do you think the presenter will say when you see each picture?

3 ▶ Watch the video to check your answers.

You can guess the meaning of many words in English if you understand the prefix (the initial part of a word). Here are some of the most common prefixes in English:

im-/un- = not: *immobile, immodest, unbelievable, unafraid*

re- = again: *review, recall, reappear*

dis- = not: *disagree, disappear*

extra- = more than: *extravagant, extraterrestrial*

sub- = under: *subdivide, subindustry*

---

4 Work with a partner. Try to work out the definitions of the words in bold. Use the box above to help you.

   1 Much of the area behind the dam will be **submerged**.

   2 It may be **impossible** to stop natural disasters.

   3 The river is **unpredictable**.

   4 This **extraordinary** engineering project.

   5 The **relocation** of 2 million people.

   6 One of the **disadvantages** is that …

5 Which two of the three options (a, b and c) make collocations with words (1–7)?

1	rich	**a** project	**b** people	**c** history
2	local	**a** people	**b** electricity	**c** area
3	surrounding	**a** heritage	**b** area	**c** buildings
4	cultural	**a** history	**b** heritage	**c** dam
5	ancient	**a** history	**b** buildings	**c** project
6	engineering	**a** buildings	**b** project	**c** industry
7	energy	**a** source	**b** people	**c** consumption

(1 b and c circled)

WHILE WATCHING

6 ▶ Watch the video. Complete the sentences with one or two words.

1 Since the Yangtze River is a major trade route, it provides _____ for the people who live along it.

2 When the river floods, it can result in the death and _____ of the local people.

3 The decision to build the Three Gorges Dam was made by the _____ .

4 The dam protects the _____ in the area below it from flooding.

5 The Yangtze can produce cheap, clean electricity as it has the world's biggest hydroelectric _____ .

6 When the dam was built, many _____ buildings, such as temples, were lost.

7 This engineering project would not have succeeded without sufficient planning and _____ .

7 ▶ Watch again. Complete the sentences below with a number from the box.

300   13   10%   3rd   2

1 The _____ longest river in the world is the Yangtze.

2 _____ million people lost their homes after a huge, destructive flood.

3 The dam also supplies _____ of the country's electricity.

4 The construction of the Three Gorges Dam involved the flooding of _____ cities.

5 The homes of _____ million people were destroyed during the construction of the dam, so these people had to be moved.

8 Work with a partner. Try to answer the questions below.

1 Overall, do you think the video gives a positive or negative view of dam building?

2 Do you think that dam building has more advantages or disadvantages?

DISCUSSION

9 Work with a partner. Discuss the questions below.

1 Do you know any large engineering projects taking place in your country at the moment?

2 What are the advantages to governments of large engineering projects? Why do governments invest in them?

3 What are the risks of investing large amounts of money in dams, bridges, airports and skyscrapers?

4 Why is it difficult to plan large engineering projects in heavily populated areas?

READING 1

PREPARING TO READ

1 Label the photographs with the words from the box.

> dam   tsunami   levee   flood barrier   sandbagging   hurricane

1 _____

2 _____

3 _____

4 _____

5 _____

6 _____

2 Skim read an interview with a disaster-mitigation expert. Decide which title below is the best and why.

1 Controlling the flow
2 The best way to protect people from flooding
3 What to do about risk
4 Protecting your house against flooding

The world has always had to face water-based natural disasters, such as tsunami and hurricanes. In an illuminating interview, Water Management Monthly talks to Dan Smith, who works in 'disaster mitigation' for a government ministry.

'Dan, could you tell us what disaster mitigation means?'

'Disaster mitigation means attempting to minimize the impact of natural disasters both before and after they happen. My department and I work in **two specific areas** in order to try and do this: risk reduction and risk analysis. They are both equally crucial in disaster mitigation.'

'What do you mean by risk reduction?'

'Risk reduction means many things. **It** is not just referring to big engineering projects like dams. Often, small community projects can be the most effective means of risk reduction. The main way floods can be prevented is by the construction and maintenance of earth wall defences, or levees. **These** block the progress of rising water. However, even the best levees can't protect against the destructive power of a tsunami. In **this case**, early-warning systems are lifesavers. They can let people know as early as possible if there is likely to be flooding.'

'What types of risk analysis do you do?'

'Firstly, risk analysis concerns flood mapping, where we identify the parts of the country which are at most risk from flooding. Secondly, there is mitigation planning, which means helping local communities plan for when disaster strikes. Thirdly, **we** make sure that the country's dams all work properly and are safe. Although many people criticize dams because of their environmental impact, there are many benefits to them too, such as hydroelectricity, irrigation, water storage, water sports and, of course, flood control. In terms of a cost-benefit analysis, we are definitely ahead.'

'Do you think countries are better prepared now for natural disasters than they were in the past?'

'Definitely. We are constantly developing new flood-prevention solutions. An example of **one such measure** can be found in the UK, with the Thames Barrier. This is an enormous engineering project designed to prevent London from flooding.'

'Aren't programmes like **that** very expensive? What lower-cost alternatives are there?'

'Flood prevention does not have to be expensive. Sandbags, for example, can be a highly effective way of stopping flood water.'

'Is there any more which can be done, or are we as prepared as we can be?'

'There's always more which could be done. But remember that the government can only be responsible for flood prevention up to a certain point. People have to become aware of the dangers of flooding themselves. This is crucial. Expensive early-warning systems are a waste of money if people take no notice of **them**.'

WHILE READING

3 Read the interview again. Are the statements below true (T), false (F) or the article does not say (DNS)?

1 Dan Smith works for an international organization. _____
2 Risk reduction and risk analysis are as important as each other in disaster mitigation. _____
3 Large-scale projects are always effective in terms of risk reduction. _____
4 Well-built defences are always successful, even against very powerful floods. _____
5 The purpose of flood mapping is to predict which areas are most likely to flood. _____
6 Planning for natural disasters has improved in recent years. _____
7 The Thames Barrier cost £20 million to build. _____
8 Low-technology solutions can protect against flooding too. _____

> Good academic writing flows easily and is not too repetitive. The writer needs to show links between ideas, but tries to avoid repeating the same words. Using pronouns and synonyms in the place of nouns and noun phrases can help. To read well in English, you need to be able to identify what these pronouns and synonyms refer to.

4 Find the words below in the interview. Write the nouns or noun phrases that they refer to.

1 two specific areas _____
2 It _____
3 These _____
4 this case _____
5 we _____
6 one such measure _____
7 that _____
8 them _____

READING BETWEEN THE LINES

5 Work with a partner. Which of the opinions below do you think Dan Smith would agree with?

1 It's the government's responsibility to protect us from natural disasters.
2 Surely it's more important to spend time and money on ways to stop water causing flooding, rather than finding out which areas are likely to flood. We already know that.
3 Dams are more trouble than they're worth.
4 The Thames Barrier was a waste of money – sandbags are just as good.
5 People in flood-risk areas need to be educated about the risks and about how they can help themselves.

DISCUSSION

6 Work with a partner. Discuss the questions below.

　1 How would life in your country be different if you had higher or lower rainfall?

　2 Does your country ever have problems with flooding? If so, how do people protect themselves?

　3 Which countries have particularly serious problems with flooding? Can you think of reasons why?

READING 2

PREPARING TO READ

1 Drought is a major problem in many parts of the world. Look at the map below and identify areas where you think drought may be common.

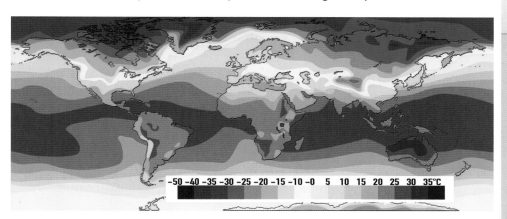

USING YOUR KNOWLEDGE TO PREDICT CONTENT

2 Work with a partner. Discuss the questions below.

　1 What are the effects of drought?

　2 How can people suffering from drought be helped in the short term?

　3 What are some long-term solutions to a shortage of water?

　4 Why do developing countries struggle with droughts?

WHILE READING

3 Match purposes (a–f) to paragraphs (1–6) in the report on the next page.

　a sets out a number of suggestions　　　　　　_____

　b considers economic factors in decision-making　_____

　c introduces the main purpose of the text　　　_____

　d discusses a range of long-term strategies　　　_____

　e discusses a range of short-term strategies　　　_____

　f briefs the reader on the effects of drought in Kenya　_____

READING FOR MAIN IDEAS

Combating drought in rural Africa: a report

1 In order to mitigate the problems which drought can bring, there are several short- and long-term strategies which can be adopted. A range of policies designed to combat these problems exist at local, national and international levels. As well as looking at these issues in general, this report will make specific recommendations in the case of Kenya, where drought has been a major problem in recent years.

2 Droughts frequently put millions of people at risk of food insecurity in central Kenya. The area is so dry that it cannot support agricultural crops. There are few permanent rivers and the seasonal waterways, which are the result of flood waters in the rainy months, disrupt transport across the region. The population of this area mainly live off their cattle. Droughts can quickly kill off their herd, leaving little or no income, and because the area is so vast, infrastructure is under-developed, meaning that access to the population is difficult.

3 When drought is predicted in central Kenya, it is important to prepare for it and be ready to respond to it as quickly as possible in order to minimize casualties. Preventive measures which may be adopted before a drought include recycling water. This is highly cost-effective. Recycled water, from the washing of clothes for example, can be given to animals and used to irrigate land. Once drought strikes, the most important short-term response is to transport bottles of drinking water into the drought area, although this is quite expensive. Since drought also often kills animals and crops, it is vital to bring food to prevent people from starving.

4 Since drought tends to reoccur in the same central areas of Kenya, long-term solutions are also necessary. Drought monitoring does not have to be expensive, and it should be possible to gather relevant data fairly cheaply, which can then be used for appropriate planning at the local and national levels. This usually involves developing irrigation systems for farming communities, or building canals and dams to benefit villages and cities. On a micro-scale, the construction of wells can help provide more water at medium cost and in reasonable timeframes. On a wider scale, desalination plants, which remove salt from sea water, also make drinking water available, but at a higher cost. Additionally, harvesting rainwater involves collecting and storing any rain that does fall. The majority of these strategies are undoubtedly expensive and may only be affordable for richer countries, which have the technology and expertise to predict and plan for drought more effectively.

5 Poorer countries, on the other hand, are generally unable to afford long-term solutions, and may have to rely on international support and charity in the short-term. Lack of education and under-developed infrastructure may also hamper some of these projects.

6 As a result of this report, the three following recommendations for Kenya are made. First, provide training in recycling and harvesting water throughout the country at a local level. Second, implement a well-construction programme, so as to maximize the amount of water available nationally. Thirdly, lobby the international community to provide funding for a desalination plant on the coast, to ensure that Kenya can always meet its water needs.

4 Read the report again. Place the strategies for dealing with drought (1–6) in the appropriate places in the diagram below.

1 constructing dams
2 rainwater harvesting
3 building wells
4 bringing in drinking water
5 water recycling
6 constructing desalination plants

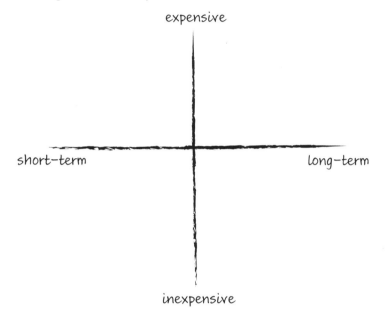

READING BETWEEN THE LINES

5 Choose the best answers.

1 What is the main purpose of this report?
  a to evaluate which solutions for drought are best globally
  b to describe a country which suffers from drought
  c to present a range of general drought solutions and focus on a specific case study
2 Why are the people of central Kenya most at risk of drought?
  a because transport is disrupted
  b their way of life means they need to use a lot of water
  c the area experiences low annual rainfall
3 Which of the points below do you think the report agrees with most?
  a High-technology solutions are always better than low-technology solutions.
  b Partnership between different organizations is important in preventing drought.
  c Every country should follow the recommendations given to Kenya in this report.

DISCUSSION

6 Work with a partner. Discuss the questions below.

1 Has your country ever experienced drought?
2 Which strategies mentioned in the text does your country use?
3 In the future, do you think that droughts across the world will be more or less severe?
4 Who should take responsibility for drought mitigation: governments, international organizations, or both?

⊙ LANGUAGE DEVELOPMENT

Academic noun phrases

Two nouns may sometimes be combined in academic writing in order to create a more complex noun phrase that gives greater detail about the subject.

    risk + analysis = risk analysis

The meaning of the more complex noun phrase will contain elements of the base nouns.

    risk = danger, threat
    analysis = the process of looking at something in detail
    risk analysis = the process of looking at dangers or threats in detail

When creating noun phrases, it may be necessary to nominalize adjectives, verbs or adverbs.

    manufacture the product = product manufacturing

1 Complete each sentence (b) with an academic noun phrase formed from words in each sentence (a).

1 a We need to mitigate these kinds of disasters.
  b We need _____ .
2 a An important component of managing natural disasters is reducing risk.
  b _____ is an important component of managing natural disasters.
3 a It is important for a country to have a system for managing water to protect against flooding.
  b It is important for a country to have a _____ _____ to protect against flooding.
4 a The report made by the government was very influential.
  b The _____ was very influential.

5 a The need for protection against floods is particularly relevant in towns located near rivers.

   b The need for _____ is particularly relevant in towns located near rivers.

6 a Projects based in the community can be very effective in minimizing risk.

   b _____ can be very effective in minimizing risk.

NATURAL DISASTER VOCABULARY

2 Look at the adjective–noun collocations below. Circle the collocation in each group which has a different meaning.

1 *natural / terrible / major* disaster
2 *severe / devastating / controlled* flood
3 *ambitious / large-scale / long-term* project
4 *prolonged / seasonal / extreme* drought

3 Complete the sentences (1–8) with a collocation from Exercise 2. In some cases, more than one answer may be possible.

1 Due to their complexity, desalination plants are _____ , which may take many years to construct.

2 One of the worst _____ in human history was the 1556 earthquake in Shaanxi province, China.

3 _____ are sometimes used to improve the quality of rivers.

4 _____ such as dams, flood defences and early warning systems require huge amounts of investment.

5 In 1931, there was a _____ in China, where more than a million people lost their lives to the water.

6 Due to a very hot climate, sub-Saharan Africa suffers from _____ more than many other places in the world.

7 In an increasing number of places, the lack of winter rain makes the chances of _____ in the summer more likely.

8 Where proper planning has been in place, the chance of a flood or drought turning into a _____ are reduced.

CRITICAL THINKING

At the end of this unit, you will write a report referring to a case study. Look at this unit's writing task in the box below.

> Write a report which provides both short- and long-term solutions to an environmental problem. Refer to a specific case study in your report.

ANALYZE

1 Read the four case studies. Match strategies (1–8) to case studies (A–D). Each strategy may be applied to several case studies.

Case study A: Fire risk

Location: Southern Australia
Geography: heavily forested areas
Country GDP rank in world: #12
Potential causes of fire: drought, human activity, global warming
Frequency: common during summer months
Effects: loss of life; destruction of homes and other buildings; destruction of habitats for wild animals; pollution from smoke

Case study B: Damage from earthquakes

Location: Haiti
Geography: island in the Caribbean
Country GDP rank in world: #138
Cause: movement of tectonic plates; lack of reinforced buildings; lack of infrastructure
Frequency: eight major earthquakes in the past 500 years
Effects: loss of life from collapsed buildings; homelessness; spread of disease; loss of infrastructure

Case study C: Dust storms

Location: Mauritania, North Africa
Geography: mainly desert
Country GDP rank in world: #154
Potential causes: wind, drought, farming practices, deforestation
Frequency: until early 1960s about two per year; since 1960s, 80 per year.
Effects: loss of fertile soil; health dangers (breathing problems); poor visibility for transport

Case study D: Flooding

Location: the Maldives
Geography: group of islands in the Indian Ocean; average 1.5 metres above sea level
Country GDP rank in world: #166
Potential cause of flooding: rising sea levels due to climate change
Potential effects: complete loss of islands, including homes of up to 320,000 people

strategies	case studies
1 Replanting suitable trees	_____
2 Educating the community about prevention and protection	_____
3 Reconstructing appropriate buildings	_____
4 Creating barriers	_____
5 Raising international awareness	_____
6 Encouraging responsible farming practices	_____
7 Installing early-warning systems	_____
8 Developing monitoring systems	_____

2 Work in groups. Discuss how these strategies could help solve the specific problems in the case studies.

3 Write strategies (1–8) in the diagram below. depending on their cost and how short- or long-term you think they are.

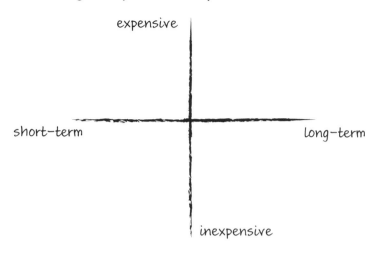

WRITING

GRAMMAR FOR WRITING

EXPLANATION

Expressing solutions using *it*

Most sentences in English need a subject as well as a verb. Look at this sentence.

Minimizing the risks caused by natural disasters is possible.

The words in bold are the subject. When the subject is long like this, it sounds better to change the sentence, so we use *it* as the subject.

It is possible to minimize the risks caused by natural disasters.

Note that *it* has no meaning in this structure. It does not refer to anything else in the text. It is only included to provide a subject for the sentence.

There are a number of grammar patterns which follow *it*.

1 *it* + *is* + noun phrase or adjective + *to* + infinitive
It is important to prepare for natural disasters.
It is a good idea to keep an emergency kit at home.

2 *it* + *is* + adjective + *-ing* form
It is worth preparing for natural disasters.

3 *it* + *is* + noun phrase or adjective + *that* + clause
It is surprising that governments do not always prepare for disasters.
It is a sad fact that many lives were lost.

1 Match the sentence halves.

1 It is important	a preparing for droughts even during the rainy season.
2 It is unlikely	
3 It is difficult	b to protect homes and businesses from floods.
4 It is worth	
5 It is not worth	c to guarantee flood protection in areas close to major rivers.
6 It is never a good idea to	
	d that a tsunami can overcome flood defences.
7 It is not surprising	e build homes in a flood zone.
8 It is not easy to	f that short-term drought solutions will work over a long period.
	g persuade people to move away from areas at risk of floods.
	h investing in tsunami warnings if people don't take notice of them.

2 Complete the sentences below with your own ideas.

1 It is important to prepare for a flood by ...
2 It is a good idea to build houses ...
3 In areas that suffer from drought, it's worth ...
4 When working with many different organizations, it can be difficult ...
5 Given how complex dam-construction projects are, it is not surprising ...
6 If there is a severe weather warning, it is ...

ACADEMIC WRITING SKILLS

PARAGRAPH STRUCTURE IN ESSAYS

1 An academic essay consists of a series of paragraphs. Which of the sentences below do you think are true about paragraphs?

1 The main purpose of paragraphs is to make the text look better on the page.
2 Paragraphs make it easier for the writer to organize his or her writing.
3 A text divided into paragraphs is easier for the reader to follow.
4 A paragraph should contain one main idea or argument.
5 The points in the paragraph should progress from specific to general.
6 There is usually a topic sentence near the beginning of the paragraph.
7 A paragraph should contain no more than two sentences.

EXPLANATION

The development of ideas in a body paragraph is extremely important. Follow the plan below to write a good paragraph.

• Topic sentence: main idea
• Explanation of main idea
• Illustration and examples of main idea

2 Put the sentences below in order to make a paragraph.

   a Another way is to harvest rainwater by collecting and storing any that does fall and using it for flushing toilets and watering the garden.

   b In very dry regions of the world, it is important to conserve as much water as possible.

   c The first step to take is to avoid any wastage of water by making sure taps are completely turned off when finished with.

   d The water from the shower, bath and washing machine can also be used for these purposes.

   e This is the cheapest and easiest way to ensure inhabitants have adequate water for their everyday needs.

3 Write a paragraph about protecting a house from a flood.

   1 Write a topic sentence.

   2 Write a sentence to explain or support your topic sentence.

   3 Write three sentences, each describing an action the householder should take before the flood arrives.

WRITING TASK

> Write a report which provides both short- and long-term solutions to an environmental problem. Refer to a specific case study in your report.

1 Complete an outline for your report below. Use a case study from the Critical thinking section or a case study from your own country.

PLAN

1 Main purpose of report

_____

2 Description of a specific case study

_____

_____

3 Short-term solutions

_____

_____

4 Long-term solutions

_____

_____

5 Summary and evaluation of key points

_____

_____

2 Complete the report using your outline. Write 250–300 words.

3 Use the task checklist to review your report for content and structure.

TASK CHECKLIST	✔
Have you used an appropriate structure for the report?	
Do your paragraphs all include topic sentences and development of ideas?	
Have you identified both short- and long-term solutions in your essay?	
Have you included relevant supporting information and examples in the essay?	
Have you referred to a case study?	
Have you written 250–300 words?	

4 Make any necessary changes to your report.

5 Now use the language checklist to edit your report for language errors which are common to B2 learners.

LANGUAGE CHECKLIST	✔
Have you used academic noun phrases where appropriate?	
Have you checked that the words in your phrases collocate correctly?	
Have you correctly used phrases with *it*, where appropriate?	
Have you spelt any environmental collocations correctly?	

6 Make any necessary changes to your report.

OBJECTIVES REVIEW

7 Check your objectives.

I can ...

watch and understand a video about the Three Gorges Dam

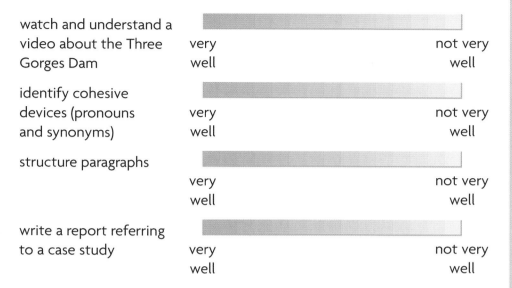

very well   not very well

identify cohesive devices (pronouns and synonyms)

very well   not very well

structure paragraphs

very well   not very well

write a report referring to a case study

very well   not very well

WORDLIST

UNIT VOCABULARY		ACADEMIC VOCABULARY
ambitious (adj)	natural (adj)	disadvantage (n)
community (n)	prolong (v)	disaster mitigation (n)
dam (n)	sandbagging (n)	extraordinary (adj)
disaster (n)	seasonal (adj)	impossible (adj)
extreme (adj)	severe (adj)	product manufacturing (n)
government report (n)	tsunami (n)	relocation (n)
hurricane (n)		risk analysis (n)
large-scale (adj)		risk reduction (n)
levee (n)		submerge (v)
long-term (adj)		unpredictable (adj)
major (adj)		

LEARNING OBJECTIVES

Watch and listen	Watch and understand a video about Islamic architecture
Reading skills	Skim read a text
Academic writing skills	Order information
Writing task	Write a persuasive essay

UNLOCK YOUR KNOWLEDGE

Work with a partner. Discuss the questions below.

1 Do people in your country generally live in houses or apartments?
2 What is the most important room in your home? Why?
3 What would you change about your home, school or workplace to improve it?
4 Are there any famous old buildings in your country? Are they protected? Do you think this is important? Why / Why not?

PREPARING TO WATCH

USING YOUR
KNOWLEDGE TO
PREDICT CONTENT

1   You are going to watch a video about Islamic architecture. Before you watch, match buildings (1–3) to three of the photographs above.

1   the Sultan Ahmed Mosque
2   the Taj Mahal
3   the Alhambra Palace

UNDERSTANDING
KEY VOCABULARY

2   Match words (1–10) to definitions (a–j).

1 emperor	**a**	a building for Muslim worship
2 tile	**b**	a place where people wash communally
3 bathhouse	**c**	a stone building or room where someone is buried
4 palace	**d**	a tall, narrow building or part of a building
5 tower	**e**	leader of an empire
6 mosque	**f**	a piece of baked clay used for covering walls
7 sultan	**g**	a type of smooth rock (often white) used in construction
8 architect	**h**	a ruler in a Muslim country
9 tomb	**i**	a large building where an important person lives
10 marble	**j**	a person who designs a building

WHILE WATCHING

UNDERSTANDING
MAIN IDEAS

3   ▶ Watch the video. Answer the questions.

1   Think of three adjectives to describe Islamic architecture.
2   Which building would you most like to visit?
3   Which building has the most interesting history? Why?

4 ▶ Watch the video again. Complete the table with details about the three buildings mentioned.

building	type	features	architect/builder
the Alhambra	Islamic (1)_____	extensive (2)_____ and fountains.	rulers of the Emirate of Granada
the Sultan Ahmed Mosque	religious (3)_____	(4)_____ tiles	(5)_____ on the walls by Ametli Kasım Gubarım
the Taj Mahal	Islamic (6)_____	decorated with paint and precious (7)_____	the Mughal Shah Jahan and (8)_____ from Turkey, Iran and Pakistan

5 ▶ Watch again. Match buildings (a–c) to details (1–9).

a the Alhambra
b the Sultan Ahmed Mosque
c the Taj Mahal

1 built by 10,000 workers _____
2 13 large towers _____
3 an iron chain at the entrance _____
4 finished in 1616 _____
5 an irrigation system _____
6 carved marble _____
7 calligraphy _____
8 in Istanbul _____
9 water channels _____

DISCUSSION

6 Work with a partner. Discuss the questions below.

1 Is it a good idea to use government money to protect ancient buildings?
2 Should members of the public pay to visit these buildings?
3 How should we choose which ancient buildings to protect and conserve?

READING 1

PREPARING TO READ

USING YOUR
KNOWLEDGE TO
PREDICT CONTENT

1 Work with a partner. Answer the questions below.

1 Which parts of buildings use the most energy?
2 Do you think it is important for new buildings to be environmentally friendly? Why / Why not?
3 How can architects design buildings to use less energy in their construction or use?
4 How can we reduce the amount of energy we use in our homes?

UNDERSTANDING
KEY VOCABULARY

2 Complete sentences (1–8) with the words in the box. Use the Glossary on page 198 to help you.

> install   straw   solar panels   efficiency   green   mud
> affordable   durable   compromise

1 Buildings which are tough and last a long time are made from _____ materials.
2 In order to minimize energy costs, modern buildings try to have high-_____ standards.
3 Environmentally friendly building methods can involve the use of traditional materials such as _____ or
_____ .
4 Environmentalists argue that architects should never _____ on quality or efficiency because of financial cost.
5 Many architects now _____ environmentally friendly systems in the buildings they design.
6 Architects usually want their buildings to be _____ and have a low impact on the environment.
7 To turn sunlight into electricity, roofs may be fitted with
_____ .
8 Some companies worry that environmentally friendly building designs are expensive and therefore not _____ .

WHILE READING

Skimming

Skimming is reading a text quickly in order to get a general idea of its main points. It is particularly useful when you have a great deal of information to read in a short space of time, or when it is not necessary to understand a text in detail. We often skim read a text to find out if it will be useful or not before reading it more thoroughly. This is particularly important in academic reading where you may only have time to read the most useful texts.

Do ...

✔ look at the title, any subheadings and illustrations – they will often give clues about the content.

✔ read the introduction, which should tell you what the text will be about.

✔ read the conclusion.

✔ read the first sentence of each paragraph, which may present its topic.

Don't ...

✘ stop to look up unknown words.

✘ say the individual words that you read in your head. Try just to focus on the meaning.

✘ read examples.

3 Look at the photographs with the article on the next page. Read the title, the introduction and the conclusion only. Choose the best answer for question 1.

SKIMMING

1 This article will be useful for a student who needs to find out about ...
  a the conservation of ancient buildings.
  b the causes of climate change.
  c typical English houses.
  d arguments for and against ecologically responsible construction.

4 How did you find the answer to question 1? Say whether the photographs, title, introduction or conclusion was most useful.

5 Skim read the article and match ideas (a–e) to paragraphs (1–5).

  a An example of a green educational establishment
  b An example of an eco-home
  c A current trend in construction
  d The certainty that we need to make changes in construction
  e The pros and cons of designing eco-buildings

Are green buildings too costly?

1 In recent years, there has been a general trend for new buildings to be more environmentally friendly. These buildings use energy and water efficiently, reducing waste and pollution. However, installing features like solar panels and water-recycling systems involves higher construction costs than in a traditional building. The question is whether customers are willing to pay these extra costs.

2 One school in the UK has shown us that ecological principles are just as relevant for small-scale projects as large-scale ones. Howe Dell primary school has its own wind turbine to generate energy, uses rainwater to flush toilets, and uses desks and sinks made from materials such as old drainpipes and yoghurt pots. These environmental aspects of the building are relatively inexpensive, and over the life of the building, should provide a large return for the initial investment. They also function as valuable teaching aids when educating students about the environment.

3 Another example of an eco-building in the UK is a private residence in Wales, known as the 'Hobbit House'. Its frame is made from wood and the walls from straw, which provides excellent insulation. The roof consists of mud planted with grass, which keeps heat in and has a low impact on the environment. Solar panels provide electricity for lighting and electrical equipment. Water is supplied directly from a nearby river and is also collected from the roof for use in the garden, therefore avoiding the need to waste clean water. Low-impact houses like this one are green because they do not rely on fossil fuels, such as oil or gas, but instead use renewable energy sources, such as solar or wind power.

4 Critics of these kinds of eco-building say that while they may be good for the environment, there are practical problems with their affordability, as they are too costly to become a large-volume method of construction. There are further concerns over their long-term efficiency. Not much energy can be realistically generated by solar panels in the UK, and not every location has access to a natural water source. In order to finance environmentally friendly construction and produce an affordable building, compromises have to be made. These may be that the building will have to be smaller or made of less durable materials and with less energy-hungry technology. Perhaps these compromises are easier to make in a school, where the green features are useful for education, or a business where ecologically-aware features are a useful marketing tool, rather than for home owners.

5 The argument for constructing green buildings is clear. The United Nations Environment Programme estimates that the construction sector accounts for 30–40% of global energy use. In some areas, such as the Gulf States, the figure is closer to 50–60%. We need to reduce this energy use for the good of the planet. However, it remains to be seen whether we are currently able to accept the financial and practical compromises of producing and living in environmentally friendly buildings.

6 Say whether architectural features (1–10) belong to Howe Dell primary school (HD), the Hobbit House (HH) or neither building (N).

1 a grass roof _____
2 a local water source _____
3 underfloor heating _____
4 a wooden construction _____
5 a wind power generator _____
6 second-hand furniture _____
7 water recycling for plants _____
8 water recycling for sanitation _____
9 natural insulation _____
10 solar-powered lighting _____

7 Read the article again. Write true (T), false (F) or does not say (DNS) next to the statements below.

1 Generally, eco-buildings are becoming more popular. _____
2 Eco-buildings cost double the price of a traditional building. _____
3 Customers do not want to pay extra for environmentally friendly houses. _____
4 Environmentally friendly practices are relevant, whatever size of building you are constructing. _____
5 Some old construction methods can be useful in terms of environmentally friendly construction. _____
6 Fossil fuels are examples of renewable types of energy. _____
7 The UK is one of the world's leading supporters of eco-buildings. _____
8 The United Nations Environment Programme produces data about global energy use. _____

READING BETWEEN THE LINES

8 Work with a partner. Try to answer the questions.

1 'In recent years there has been a general trend for new buildings to be more environmentally friendly.' Why do you think this is?
2 The environmental aspects of the school 'also function as valuable teaching aids when educating students about the environment'. What do you think students learn?
3 'Not much energy can be realistically generated by solar panels in the UK.' Why not?
4 Why can environmentally friendly aspects of a business be 'a useful marketing tool'?

DISCUSSION

9 Work with a partner. Discuss the questions below.

1 Would you live in an eco-home if you had to pay more for its environmentally friendly features? Why / Why not?
2 Do you think there should be restrictions on how much energy individuals or institutions should be allowed to use? Why / Why not?

USING YOUR
KNOWLEDGE TO
PREDICT CONTENT

PREPARING TO READ

1 Work with a partner. Discuss the questions below.

1 Which are the most beautiful buildings in your country?
2 Are these buildings older traditional buildings or modern constructions?
3 Do people in your country generally prefer to live in modern or older houses?
4 What do people in your country think about modern architecture?
5 Which is more important when designing a building: its beauty or its function?

2 Skim read the essay. Does the writer think it is more important to design a building which is beautiful or one which is functional?

WHILE READING

READING FOR
MAIN IDEAS

3 Read the essay again and complete the summary below.

While some architecture values (1)_____ over form, there is an opposing view that the (2)_____ of a building is more important than its functionality. In practice, most (3)_____ strive for a combination of both ideas.

The first consideration in the design of a (4)_____ should be its purpose. The physical space should allow its (5)_____ to function as efficiently and comfortably as possible.

Architects should also aim to design attractive buildings, as this can impact on the users' (6)_____ and hence motivation. The appearance of a building can also (7)_____ , either positively or negatively, on its owner.

(8)_____ form and function is obviously the ideal, but it is not always so easy to achieve, as shortcomings in several (9)_____ buildings have shown.

Which is more important when designing a building: beauty or function?

At the start of the twentieth century, Louis Sullivan, one of the creators of modern architecture, said that 'form follows function'. 'Functionalism' is used to describe the idea behind architecture which primarily focuses on the purpose of a building. However, many people disagree with this and feel that beauty is a more important factor in architectural design. In the modern world, it seems that most architects combine both ideas: aiming to create buildings which are both functional and beautiful.

The reason for creating a building in the first place is clearly very important. For example, when building an airport terminal, you need to think of the needs of passengers as well as planes. Passengers want to get to their plane as quickly as they can, and planes need to be parked in the most efficient way possible. As such, many airport terminals have a circular shape with satellite areas. Residential homes need to have enough space for a family, art galleries need wall space to show pictures, and factories need to produce goods as efficiently as possible. Each type of building has a different function and hence a different form.

Beauty, however, is also clearly important when constructing a building. Living or working in an ugly place creates a depressing and uninspiring environment. In contrast, an attractive building can make people feel happier and increase their motivation to work. There is also a wider responsibility to society which architects have to consider. Beautiful, well-constructed buildings are a symbol of a civilized society and reflect well on the business or reputation of the owner. Ugly public buildings, however, can project a negative image of the organization.

In theory, there seems to be no reason why architecture cannot be both functional and beautiful. Yet in practice, this can cause problems. The Modern International style of the 1920s and 1930s, an example of which is the Guggenheim Museum in New York, was supposed to combine beauty with function. Many consider the museum's white spiral ramp beautiful, but there have been complaints that it is impractical, as it is difficult to stand back to view the art. Also, the ramp is so narrow that it can become overcrowded. The Farnsworth House by Ludwig Mies van der Rohe is another icon of beautiful, functional design that demonstrates the idea that 'less is more'. However, critics have attacked it for a lack of privacy because of the huge glass windows. It also has a leaky flat roof and has been repeatedly flooded. It seems that even these two celebrated designs have problems with functionality.

The Guggenheim Museum

If architects focus only on function, buildings may be cold, ugly and uninteresting. On the other hand, if they focus only on making it look beautiful, the building may be completely impractical. Therefore, blending these two ideas is necessary to create the perfect piece of architecture.

The Farnsworth House

4 Match the original sentences (1–6) from the text to the correct paraphrases (a–f).

1 Beautiful, well-constructed buildings are a symbol of a civilized society.
2 Living or working in an ugly place creates a depressing and uninspiring environment.
3 There is also a wider responsibility to society which architects have to consider.
4 'Less is more'.
5 Even these two celebrated designs have problems with functionality.
6 Each type of building has a different function and hence a different form.

a Buildings which are not beautiful can make people feel unhappy and bored.
b Attractive, safe buildings represent a cultured society.
c A minimalist design can actually create a more powerful effect.
d Every construction has a different purpose, and is therefore designed according to different criteria.
e These famous buildings may have won awards but they still do not always fulfil users' needs.
f People who design buildings have a duty to the general public.

READING BETWEEN THE LINES

MAKING INFERENCES
FROM THE TEXT

5 Work with a partner. Try to answer the questions below.

1 Why are well-designed buildings advantageous for the owner?
2 Why is a circular or satellite shape beneficial for an airport terminal?
3 Why might governments demolish ugly public buildings?
4 What elements of a building could make it depressing?
5 Why could the design of a building increase your motivation?

DISCUSSION

6 Work with a partner. Discuss the questions below.

1 Would you like to live in the Farnsworth House? Why? / Why not?
2 How would you design your own home if money were no object?
3 Do you agree that architects have a 'wider responsibility' to society, or should they just do what their client wants?
4 After reading the article, do you have an opinion about whether function or form is more important?

◎ LANGUAGE DEVELOPMENT

EXPLANATION

Academic word families

When you learn new words, you should also try and learn other words in the same word family. If you learn the noun *combination*, you should also try and learn the verb (*combine*) and adjective (*combined*).

Architects aim for a **combination** of beauty and functionality. (noun)
Architects should **combine** beauty and functionality. (verb)
The **combined** beauty and functionality make this a perfect building. (adjective)

1 Complete the word families in the table below.

noun	verb	adjective	adverb
function, functionalism	function	functional	functionally
environment		(1)_____	(2)_____
(3)_____	(4)_____	depressing	(5)_____
responsibility		(6)_____	(7)_____
architect, (8)_____		(9)_____	(10)_____
(11)_____		(12)_____	efficiently

2 Complete the sentences below with words from the table in Exercise 1.

1 It is important to consider the _____ impact of any new building.
2 _____ is an architectural system which believes that function is more important than beauty.
3 Environmentally friendly buildings are usually very _____ .
4 Architects need to plan buildings _____ in order to ensure that they are sustainable.
5 Badly designed buildings can _____ even the happiest person.
6 One famous critic described _____ as 'frozen music'.
7 Architects must consider the impact of buildings on the
   _____ .
8 Employers must be _____ for providing healthy working areas.
9 Badly built office buildings may cause _____ in workers.
10 Certain details of _____ styles change all the time, but most key principles remain the same.

ARCHITECTURE AND PLANNING VOCABULARY

3 Complete the definitions below with the words from the box. Use the Glossary on page 198 to help you.

> structural engineer   conservation   skyscrapers   outskirts
> green belt   urban sprawl   amenities

1 A person whose job it is to help build an architect's design is a
_____ .
2 _____ are very tall modern buildings.
3 When cities spread out into the countryside, _____
_____ may be the result.
4 The _____ is a band of unspoilt countryside which may not be built on.
5 The suburbs are found on the _____ of a city.
6 It is important that governments make _____ like libraries and sports facilities available for everybody.
7 Many believe that the _____ of ancient buildings is important.

4 Complete the sentences below with your own ideas.

1 The key responsibility of an architect is ...
2 When building skyscrapers, it is important ...
3 Conservation may be expensive, but ...
4 Green belt land is important because ...
5 Important amenities which should be provided by the government include ...
6 Urban sprawl has a negative effect on the environment because ...

CRITICAL THINKING

At the end of this unit, you will write a persuasive essay. Look at this unit's writing task in the box below.

> Which is more important when building or buying a new home: its location or its size?

1 Read arguments (1–6) and circle (a, b or c).
   a = the environment is more important
   b = minimizing cost is more important
   c = both are equally important
   1 The construction company has to make a profit, so it
     should construct buildings cheaply.   a   b   c
   2 Eco-buildings may encourage people to be more
     environmentally responsible in their day-to-day lives.   a   b   c
   3 Environmentally friendly buildings cost less in the long
     run, due to energy savings.   a   b   c
   4 Due to global population increase, we urgently need
     more buildings; if they are expensive, they are less likely
     to be built.   a   b   c
   5 Cheaply constructed buildings have a shorter lifespan
     and may need to be destroyed sooner.   a   b   c
   6 Government grants may be available for eco-buildings.   a   b   c

2 Place arguments (1–6) from Exercise 1 on the lines below, depending on
  how persuasive you think they are.

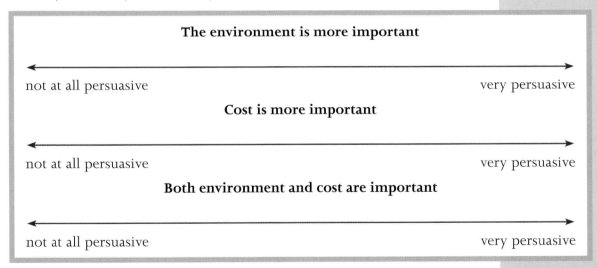

The environment is more important

not at all persuasive   very persuasive

Cost is more important

not at all persuasive   very persuasive

Both environment and cost are important

not at all persuasive   very persuasive

3 Look at the writing task. Put a cross on the line below according
  to your opinion. Then compare your answer with a partner. Discuss
  your opinions.

> Which is more important when designing a building: its impact on the
> environment or its cost?

Cost is the only thing   Environmental concerns are
that matters.   the only things that matter.

WRITING

GRAMMAR FOR WRITING

Register in academic writing

The types of language used in informal writing and formal, academic written English are very different. Informal language tends to be similar to speaking, whereas in formal written English, we usually use the following:

- longer, more complex sentences
- more precise, technical words
- more formal phrases and linking words.

Whereas we usually avoid the following:

- slang and colloquial expressions
- phrasal verbs (unless there is no alternative word)
- first person personal pronouns (*I* and *me*).

1 Match informal words/phrases (1–9) in the text below to academic words/phrases (a–i).

> Choosing an architect is (1)**basically** about cost for many organizations. (2)**I am sure that** regardless of whether the building is for the private or public sector, initial cost is (3)**really important**. Good architecture requires (4)**lots of money**, and institutions have to (5)**work out** whether high costs (6)**are worth it** in the long term. Some people claim that (7)**there's not much point** in providing an attractive working area. However, others would argue that a pleasant working environment (8)**is good for** people's moods and therefore their productivity. A recent survey in a multinational IT company suggested that (9)**around about** 75% of employees took this view.

a calculate
b can be justified
c fundamentally
d approximately
e there is no real benefit

f considerable investment
g has a positive impact on
h critical
i undoubtedly

2 Complete the sentences below with your own ideas.

1 Fundamentally, good buildings are those that …
2 It is difficult to calculate …
3 One thing which is critical when designing new buildings is …
4 The installation costs of solar panels can only be justified if …
5 Architecture can have a positive impact on …
6 There is no real benefit in …

ACADEMIC WRITING SKILLS

Ordering information

To make writing fluent, we often refer back to the previous sentence when it has the same topic. Look at the examples:

When choosing a new house, the most important consideration may be (location.) (Areas near good schools) are often popular.
For many people the first criterion is (size.) (The number of bedrooms) may be determined by family size.

In the examples above, the beginning of the second sentence is a paraphrase of the end of the first one. Sometimes we just use a reference word, such as *this*, *that*, *these*, *those* or reference phrases like *That is why*, *For this reason*, *In spite of this*.

Some families prefer to extend their existing houses. **This** allows all family members to live together.
Living in a city centre can mean parking problems. **In spite of this,** many people are drawn to urban areas.

1 Read each sentence (1–5) in bold. Then decide which follow-up sentence (a or b) sounds more appropriate.

1 **Small homes can be crowded.**
   a This lack of space can cause family tensions.
   b We should live in large houses so everybody has plenty of space.

2 **Homes should be near shops and schools.**
   a Fuel costs can be saved if we do not have to drive.
   b Being able to access these amenities without a car is a bonus.

3 **It is better to live in spacious buildings**.
   a Large open rooms allow families to spend more time together.
   b People can spend more time together if they have large open rooms.

4 **A small apartment is suitable for a small family.**
   a However, if parents subsequently have more children, they may need to move again.
   b A small apartment is not a good idea for those planning to have a large family.

5 **Ideally, we need homes that are convenient for travelling to work.**
   a Accessibility is an important everyday need.
   b We often cannot choose to live near our workplace.

WRITING TASK

Which is more important when building or buying a new home: its location or its size?

1 Make notes for the essay above. In paragraphs 2 and 3 put your arguments in order of how persuasive you think they are.

Paragraph 1: Introduction
Paragraph 2: Arguments in favour of location being more important

_____

_____

_____

Paragraph 3: Arguments in favour of size being more important

_____

_____

_____

Paragraph 4: Your position and conclusions

_____

_____

_____

2 Write your essay. Write 250–300 words.

3 Use the task checklist to review your essay for content and structure.

TASK CHECKLIST	✔
Does your essay follow the structure provided?	
Do your arguments reflect both sides of the question?	
Have you prioritized your arguments in order of how persuasive you think they are?	
Do your examples adequately support your ideas?	
Have you written between 250–300 words?	

4 Make any necessary changes to your essay.

5 Now use the language checklist to edit your essay for language errors which are common to B2 learners.

LANGUAGE CHECKLIST	✔
Have you spelt different words from the same word family correctly?	
Have you used subject-specific language correctly?	
Have you used formal academic language throughout?	
Does any referencing to subjects in previous sentences use pronouns correctly?	

6 Make any necessary changes to your essay.

OBJECTIVES REVIEW

7 Check your objectives.

I can ...

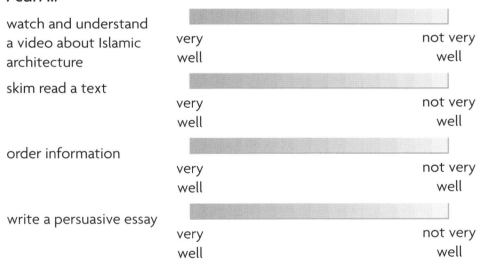

watch and understand a video about Islamic architecture

very well   not very well

skim read a text

very well   not very well

order information

very well   not very well

write a persuasive essay

very well   not very well

WORDLIST

UNIT VOCABULARY			ACADEMIC VOCABULARY	
affordable (adj)	green belt (n)	straw (n)	architectural (adj)	functionalism (n)
amenities (n)	install (v)	structural	architecture (n)	responsible (adj)
architect (n)	marble (n)	engineer (n)	depress (v)	responsibly (adv)
bathhouse (n)	mosque (n)	sultan (n)	depression (n)	
compromise (v)	mud (n)	tile (n)	efficiency (n)	
conservation (n)	outskirts (n)	tomb (n)	efficient (adj)	
durable (adj)	palace (n)	tower (n)	environment (n)	
emperor (n)	skyscraper (n)	urban sprawl (n)	environmental	
green (adj)	solar panel (n)		(adj)	

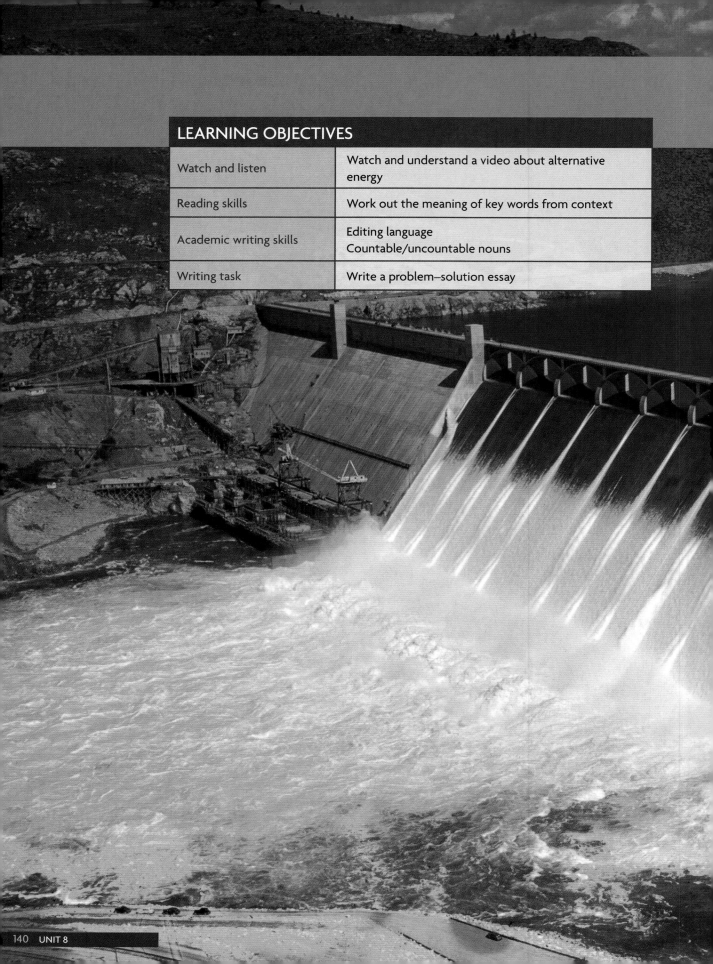

LEARNING OBJECTIVES

Watch and listen	Watch and understand a video about alternative energy
Reading skills	Work out the meaning of key words from context
Academic writing skills	Editing language Countable/uncountable nouns
Writing task	Write a problem–solution essay

UNLOCK YOUR KNOWLEDGE

Work with a partner. Discuss the questions below.

1 Do you think in general we use more energy now than we did ten years ago? Why / Why not?
2 What are fossil fuels? What is renewable energy?
3 Would you be willing to pay a much higher bill if the energy company invested in solar or wind energy? Why / Why not?
4 Is it a good idea to rely on energy from other countries?

WATCH AND LISTEN

PREPARING TO WATCH

1 Match words (1–7) to definitions (a–g).

1 petrol
2 hydroelectricity
3 solar power
4 diesel
5 canola oil
6 wind turbine
7 biofuel

a a type of heavy oil used as fuel
b a liquid made from petroleum and used as fuel
c a type of rapeseed oil which can be used as a biofuel
d a process which produces electricity from the sun
e a fuel that is made from the waste of living things
f a process which produces electricity from fast-moving water
g a tall structure which generates electricity from fast-moving air

2 You are going to watch a video about renewable energy. Before you watch, write the words from Exercise 1 in the correct columns below.

fossil fuels	renewable energy

WHILE WATCHING

3 ▶ Watch the video and answer the questions.

1 Which two forms of renewable energy does it focus on?
2 Does the video discuss their advantages, disadvantages or both?
3 Does it discuss national or local projects or both?

UNDERSTANDING MAIN IDEAS

4 ▶ Watch the video again and answer the questions below.

1 What two reasons are given for why we need to find sources of clean, renewable energy?
2 How did one community help itself?
3 What advantages of biofuels are mentioned?
4 What is the 'huge challenge' that faces most countries?

LISTENING FOR KEY INFORMATION

5 ▶ Watch again. Complete the summary below.

In Mount Pleasant, Washington, the (1)_____ worked together so they could (2)_____ from using solar energy. The residents are also free to (3)_____ unused energy back to the supplier. Some residents have saved up to (4)_____ % on their electricity bills. To reduce the transport carbon footprint as effectively as possible, an alternative energy source for (5)_____ is required. Petrol and diesel can be replaced with (6)_____ , which is often produced from (7)_____ flowers. Since the amount of carbon dioxide they produce when burnt is the same as the amount they absorb while growing, they are carbon (8)_____ .

6 Work with a partner. What do you think the words in bold below mean?

1 modified energy **consumption**
2 **alternative** forms of power
3 the neighbourhood formed a **cooperative**
4 reducing our **carbon footprint**
5 biofuels can be **carbon neutral**

WORKING OUT MEANING FROM CONTEXT

DISCUSSION

7 Work with a partner. Discuss the questions below.

1 Why should countries try to use less energy?
2 Are there any alternative energy projects in your country? What do you know about them?
3 How can energy consumption be reduced where you live?

READING 1

PREPARING TO READ

UNDERSTANDING KEY VOCABULARY

1 Match types of alternative energy (1–5) to sources (a–e). Use a dictionary to help you.

1	hydropower	a	the sun
2	wind	b	the heat in the ground
3	solar	c	rivers
4	biomass	d	fast-moving air
5	geothermal	e	organic rubbish and waste products

2 Read the presentation slides and choose the best title for the whole presentation.

1 Why are fossil fuels running out?
2 The disadvantages of clean energy generation
3 An overview of renewable energy production
4 The benefits of alternative energy sources
5 The pros and cons of environmental conservation

Hydropower:

- *Process*: The pressure of moving water turns turbines that create energy. Hydropower may use rivers, waterfalls or the sea.
- *Main advantages*: inexhaustible; energy can be stored and used when demand is highest
- *Main disadvantages*: can have environmental impact on aquatic life; expensive initial construction costs; areas may need to be flooded if dams are built

---

Wind:

- *Process*: Large turbines are placed on top of hills or offshore. The wind turns the blades and energy is generated.
- *Main advantages*: relatively cheap; zero pollution; can be used on small or large scale
- *Main disadvantages*: many people consider wind turbines ugly and noisy; if it is not windy, no energy is produced; can be a threat to birds and wildlife

---

Solar:

- *Process*: Solar panels absorb sunlight and, using photovoltaic cells, turn it into electricity.
- *Main advantages*: inexhaustible; zero pollution; can be adapted to work on a variety of buildings / in a variety of environments
- *Main disadvantages*: large areas of land needed for production; can only be used in sunny parts of the world; can only operate for certain times of the day; cells fragile and easily damaged

Biomass:

- *Process*: Rubbish such as wood, animal waste and ethanol fuels are burned, generating steam to turn turbines.
- *Main advantages*: inexhaustible; efficient; universally available; reduces landfill
- *Main disadvantages*: contributes to global warming; expensive; ineffective on a small scale

Geothermal:

- *Process*: Heat trapped in the ground can be converted into steam to turn turbines.
- *Main advantages*: zero pollution; inexhaustible; simple technology; low running costs
- *Main disadvantages*: high installation costs; only available in certain geographical areas

WHILE READING

3 Read the slides again. Which type of alternative energy is being described in the sentences below (1–8)?

READING FOR DETAIL

1 A versatile source of energy which will last forever, but which cannot work 24 hours a day. _____
2 A type of energy which produces greenhouse gases, but which disposes of waste. _____
3 A type of energy based on steam-powered turbines, which is expensive to set up, but cheap to operate. _____
4 A type of energy which may require people to relocate. _____
5 A type of energy which may be more common or relevant in countries with deserts or which are near the equator. _____
6 A type of energy which is expensive to begin with, although the technology is relatively basic. _____
7 A type of energy which may kill wildlife or place boats in danger. _____
8 A type of energy which is efficient and which can be released as required. _____

4 Match the newspaper headlines below to an energy source.

1 Wave-power machines struggle to cope with harsh marine environment _____
2 Rare eagle struck by newly constructed turbine _____
3 Report shows that 10,000 kg of waste used last year to fuel energy plant _____
4 Amazing summer weather creates energy bonanza! _____
5 Government pledges millions for new steam-powered turbines _____
6 Low rainfall suggests high electricity prices _____
7 Environmentalists question renewable credentials of bio-energy source _____

READING BETWEEN THE LINES

When you read a word you do not understand in a text, you could look in a dictionary, but this will make your reading very slow and you may forget what you were reading. An alternative strategy is to try to guess the meaning from the context. Often you do not need the exact meaning of the word to be able to understand the sentence. To guess the meaning of an unknown word, look at the words before and after it. Look for clues to the meaning.

- Can you use logic and your knowledge of the world to guess?
  Days without sun are **rare** in the desert.

- Is the word explained in the text or are examples given?
  The nest of an **eagle**, one of the world's largest hunting birds, was destroyed when building the power station.

- Do linking words or conjunctions help you to guess?
  Although the government has **pledged** to build a new wind farm, some believe this will not happen.

5 Circle the synonym in each group which is closest in meaning to the word in bold.

1	rubbish	*leftovers / ruins / waste*
2	aquatic	*found in water / on land / in the air*
3	offshore	*underground / in the sea / on the beach*
4	inexhaustible	*unlimited / polluting / tiring*
5	initial	*subsequent / original / unusual*
6	generate	*produce / cause / begin*
7	universally	*somewhere / everywhere / nowhere*
8	store	*acquire / supply / keep*

DISCUSSION

6 Work with a partner. Discuss the questions below.

1 Which types of renewable energy could be used as an alternative to fossil fuels in your country?

2 Nuclear power is also sometimes suggested as an alternative to fossil fuels. What are the problems with using nuclear power?

3 How will the growing global population affect the type of energy sources which can be used?

4 What is more important when considering energy use: cost or impact on the environment?

READING 2

PREPARING TO READ

USING YOUR KNOWLEDGE TO PREDICT CONTENT

1 What will happen when the world starts to run out of the natural resources below?

1 oil _prices will rise; plastic, chemicals and petrol will be more expensive_

2 water _____

3 trees _____

4 food _____

5 metal _____

2 How can we tackle the problem of resource shortages?

1 oil _invest in renewable fuels like wind energy or solar power_

2 water _____

3 trees _____

4 food _____

5 metal _____

3 Work in pairs. You are going to read an essay which discusses an energy-conservation strategy called 'reduce, reuse, recycle'. Discuss what you think this means. Think of examples of what we can reduce, reuse or recycle.

4 Read the essay on the next page and check your answers.

WHILE READING

5 Match the words to make collocations.

1	alarming	a	transport
2	electrical	b	action
3	motorized	c	practices
4	wasteful	d	a strategy
5	address	e	rate
6	urgent	f	items
7	adopt	g	the problem

6 Complete the sentences (1–7) with the collocations from Exercise 5.

1 Individuals, organizations and governments can _____ such as 'reduce, reuse, recycle'.

2 It is difficult to discourage people from using _____ frequently for travelling.

3 Perhaps the only way to change people's _____ is to reward them financially.

The world is running out of many vital natural resources. Discuss the most effective ways to address this problem.

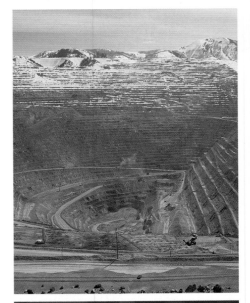

The world's natural resources are being used at an alarming rate, not only fossil fuels such as coal, oil and gas, but also water, wood, metals and minerals. This has many potential consequences for the billions of people who live on Earth. In recent years, both individuals and governments have become more interested in better managing the world's resources. To achieve this, the phrase 'reduce, reuse, recycle' is often presented as a strategy with which to approach these problems.

The main idea behind reducing the amount of resources we use is clear: namely that each individual should use less. This can be achieved by being more aware of our day-to-day resource use, such as reducing the number of electrical items on standby, using less water and avoiding motorized transport. In addition, we can introduce energy-saving mechanisms into the household: energy-saving light bulbs and water meters, for example. It is difficult to persuade people to use less energy and water, or to eat less food, but the most effective way to motivate people to change wasteful practices is to make these essential commodities much more expensive.

Reusing objects is another strategy for addressing the problem of resource use. As the name suggests, reuse is when old, unwanted items are restored to a state in which they can be used again for a similar purpose. So glass bottles, for instance, can be cleaned and reused without having to be broken and remade. Reusing things is a very efficient process and consumes much less energy than recycling. It does, however, often require a lot of expensive organization and administration. There are also concerns about reusing medical equipment and food-storage items, for example, because of safety and hygiene issues.

Recycling is the third and probably best-known option for conserving natural resources. Materials such as paper and plastic can be turned into new products, which are then reused. This process involves lower energy usage and greenhouse gas emissions than producing articles from raw materials would. However, sorting through used materials before recycling them is a dirty and difficult job and breaking up electronic equipment to recycle rare metals is time-consuming and potentially dangerous.

To avoid a catastrophic depletion of vital natural resources in the future, urgent action is required now. The 'reduce, reuse and recycle' strategy is certainly a manageable and memorable one that can be practised by individuals as well as larger organizations and even governments. However, persuading people to consistently adopt the strategy is difficult and it will need to be used alongside the development of alternative resources.

4 The 'reduce, reuse and recycle' strategy is one way to
_____ of over-consumption.

5 Unless we take _____ , we could find ourselves
without vital natural resources that we take for granted today.

6 We cannot continue using up resources at such an

_____ .

7 We should turn _____ off completely when we are
not using them.

READING BETWEEN THE LINES

7 Work with a partner. Try to answer the questions below, based on ideas
in the essay.

MAKING INFERENCES
FROM THE TEXT

1 Why will energy need to become more expensive before people are
motivated to reduce the energy they use?
2 Why should we avoid the use of motorized transport?
3 Why is reusing more efficient than recycling?
4 Why is urgent action needed to protect the world and its future
inhabitants?

DISCUSSION

8 Work with a partner. Discuss the questions below.

1 Is recycling common in your country? What objects can be recycled?
2 Do you think it is fair to penalize people financially if they do not
recycle? Can you think of any other objects that can be reused,
without having to recycle them?
3 Which of the three strategies to conserve resources mentioned above
do you think is most effective?
4 What impact might our current energy use have on future generations?

◉ LANGUAGE DEVELOPMENT

ENERGY COLLOCATIONS

1 Match the nouns in the box to the correct group of words (1–6).

> energy   problem   production   source   pollution   fuel

1 fossil / diesel / alternative / renewable / clean   _____
2 renewable / green / nuclear / solar / geothermal   _____
3 environmental / air / industrial / water / radioactive   _____
4 energy / fuel / power / water / renewable   _____
5 electricity / energy / oil / gas / agricultural   _____
6 serious / health / environmental / major / medical   _____

2 Complete the sentences below using energy collocations from Exercise 1.

1 Critics of _____ energy say that the risks to the environment outweigh the benefits of cheap electricity.

2 Asthma and diabetes are examples of increasingly common _____ problems.

3 For a renewable _____ of electricity to be truly successful, governments have to invest more money in it.

4 _____ fuels, such as oil and gas, have a finite lifespan.

5 _____ energy, whichever renewable source it comes from, tends to be slightly more expensive for the end user.

6 Rivers and lakes are two major _____ sources which can be used for hydroelectric power.

7 Hot, sunny countries are the best places to try and implement _____ energy programmes.

8 The fear that many people have about nuclear power stations is _____ pollution.

FORMAL AND INFORMAL ACADEMIC VERBS

3 Match formal verbs (1–8) with informal alternatives (a–h).

1	consult	a	get
2	contest	b	skip
3	deliver	c	start
4	diminish	d	look at
5	instigate	e	use
6	omit	f	decrease
7	secure	g	give
8	utilize	h	disagree with

4 Complete the sentences (1–8) with the correct form of the formal verbs in Exercise 3.

1 Our resources are beginning to _____ and soon they will be exhausted.

2 This company needs to _____ its energy policy to the government by the end of the year.

3 The application to construct a wind farm in this area has been _____ by local residents, who dislike the idea.

4 If people _____ the documents on our website, they can see how biofuel is made.

5 The recent rise in fuel prices should _____ a debate on oil reserves.

6 This car _____ fuel more effectively than previous models.

7 Advocates of biofuels sometimes _____ key details like how much land is needed to cultivate the crops.

8 This country needs to _____ new sources of renewable energy soon.

CRITICAL THINKING

At the end of this unit, you will write a problem–solution essay. Look at this unit's writing task below.

> The world is unable to meet its energy needs. What three sources of renewable energy would be most effective in solving this problem in your country? Which is your preferred option?

1 Read the questionnaire. Answer each question, and give a reason for your answer. Also say how this relates to your own country.

EVALUATE

	Yes/No	reason and how it relates to your country
Hydropower		
Do you think that hydropower has a negative impact on wildlife?		
Hydropower is expensive to build at first. Does this matter?		
Some areas may need to be flooded when constructing hydropower stations. Do the benefits outweigh the costs?		
Wind		
Does it matter that some people think wind turbines are ugly and noisy?		
Wind turbines can be a threat to bird life and shipping. Do the benefits outweigh the costs?		
Solar		
Large areas of land are needed for the most efficient use of solar panels. Do you feel this is a long-term problem?		
Biomass		
Biomass produces a lot of greenhouse gases. Are there more advantages than disadvantages to this energy source?		
Geothermal		
This energy source has high installation costs. Does this mean that geothermal stations should not be built?		

2 Compare your answers with a partner. Do his/her answers provide you with any extra information?

When planning an essay, you should collect the points you wish to make and then organize them. Put them in order of importance, usefulness or interest.

3 Rank the alternative sources of energy below according to which you think is best (1 = most desirable and 5 = least desirable) for your country. Compare your answers with a partner.

- hydropower _____
- wind _____
- solar _____
- biomass _____
- geothermal _____

4 Focus on your top three sources of energy. Write a sentence for each one, saying why you think it would be a suitable alternative-energy choice for your country. Use ideas from Readings 1 and 2 to help you.

rank	type of energy	reason
	example: nuclear	Nuclear power offers clean and efficient energy and the risks of accidents are small, despite people's fears. It does not require a particular climate.
1		
2		
3		

WRITING

GRAMMAR FOR WRITING

Relative clauses

In the sentence below, the part in bold is a relative clause.

Energy sources **which produce greenhouse gases** should not be used.

A relative clause is a part of a sentence that gives more information about the subject before it. In this sentence the subject is *energy sources*.

Relative clauses always start with a relative pronoun (*who* for people, *which/ that* for things or ideas, *when* for time, *where* for places, *whose* for possession). A relative clause must contain a verb.

1 Highlight the relative clause in each sentence below and write the correct relative pronoun. What does each relative clause refer to?

   1 Enrico Fermi, _____ first split the atom, is often considered the inventor of nuclear power.
   2 The people _____ houses are near nuclear power stations understandably worry about radioactive leaks.
   3 The cupboard _____ the electricity meter is located is locked.
   4 It is sometimes cheaper to use electricity at night _____ fewer people are using it.
   5 Ethanol, _____ is a type of biofuel, is made from the sugar in certain crops.

EXPLANATION

There are two kinds of relative clause: defining and non-defining.

Defining relative clauses

   Wind turbines **which are offshore** are dangerous to shipping.

The defining clause here makes it clear which subject we are talking about (the offshore wind turbines, not the ones on land). If we removed this clause from the sentence, it would suggest that all wind turbines are dangerous to shipping, even the ones on land. So, the relative clause defines the wind turbines we mean.

Non-defining relative clauses

   Wind turbines, **which may be offshore**, provide clean, renewable energy.

In this sentence, the most important information is that wind turbines provide clean, renewable energy. The relative clause provides extra information. It does not define the subject (= wind turbines in general) but provides extra information about some of them (i.e. they may be offshore). If we delete this clause, the rest of the sentence still makes sense. We put non-defining relative clauses between commas.

2 Add commas to the sentences which contain non-defining relative clauses.

   1 Nuclear power stations which have poor safety records should be closed down.
   2 Solar power which is a form of renewable energy is very popular in southern Spain.
   3 There are certain solar panels that can produce almost a kilowatt of electricity per day.
   4 Wind turbines which are located offshore are more expensive than wind turbines which are located on top of hills.
   6 People who criticize nuclear power should consult the facts.
   7 Al Gore who is a key supporter of alternative energy won the Nobel prize in 2007.

Phrases to introduce advantages and disadvantages

We can use a range of phrases to introduce the advantages and disadvantages of ideas or solutions to problems.

> One **major** advantage of ... is
> The **most obvious** advantages of ... are
> One **other apparent** advantage of ... is
> A **further possible** advantage of ... is
>
> The **most serious** disadvantage of ... is
> A **distinct** disadvantage of ... is
> One **other inherent** disadvantage of ... is
> Another **potential** disadvantage of ... is

Notice how we use adjectives like **apparent**, **possible** and **potential** to show less certain or less obvious advantages and disadvantages.

3 Use the prompts below to create sentences. Use the phrases in the box above to help you.

1 advantage, wind power, inexhaustible, never run out
   One advantage of wind power is that it is inexhaustible, so it will never run out.
2 disadvantage, biomass, produces, greenhouse gases
3 disadvantage, biomass, large areas, land, needed
4 advantage, hydropower, energy, stored, used, needed
5 disadvantage, geothermal, available, certain places
6 advantage, wind power, zero pollution
7 advantage, wind power, relatively cheap

ACADEMIC WRITING SKILLS

Editing language

Developing good editing skills is important for success in academic writing. You should carefully check and improve your work before you submit it. One of the most common errors for students at B2 level is missing out smaller words such as articles (*a*, *the*) and prepositions (*in*, *on*, *at*, *of*, *from*, *about*).

1 Complete the text with the missing prepositions. There may be more than one possible answer.

One (1)_____ the largest problems (2)_____ nuclear power is that it is potentially very dangerous. If we look (3)_____ the disaster which occurred (4)_____ Fukushima (5)_____ 11th March 2011, we can see how the land, air and sea were contaminated (6)_____ radioactive material. The government was particularly worried that clouds of radioactive gas would move (7)_____ centres of urban population. This would be particularly dangerous if the wind came (8)_____ the wrong direction. (9)_____ the Chernobyl explosion in 1986, people have been talking (10)_____ this particular issue.

EXPLANATION

Accurate spelling is important because the reader will lose confidence in your ideas if there are too many errors. Language exams also test spelling in their writing, listening and reading papers, so checking your work carefully for mistakes is good practice.

2 Find three spelling mistakes in each sentence.

1 Unclear power poses a serious proplem for the enviroment.
2 It is nuclear wich tipe of alternative energy is best.
3 To many peepul nowdays are not responsible enough in their energy usage.
4 Not enouf people now how they can improve there behaviour.
5 Bye leading confortable lives, people may be endangering futur generations.
6 Alternativ energy is much friendlier to the environment then fossil fuels becouse it is renewable.
7 It is belived that the place were solar energy wood be most effective is the Sahara.
8 Goverments won't change their policies untill there is demand form people.

COUNTABLE/UNCOUNTABLE NOUNS

3 Match uncountable nouns (1–8) to countable nouns (a–h).

1 accommodation   a tool
2 furniture   b bag
3 research   c flat/house
4 luggage   d program
5 software   e chair
6 equipment   f academic paper
7 feedback   g comment
8 stuff   h thing

4 Complete the sentences with the correct forms of the words from Exercise 3. There is sometimes more than one possible answer.

1 How much _____ can be taken on the aeroplane?
2 Did you get _____ from your teacher on your essay?
3 How many new computer_____ did you download?
4 Google Scholar says that 208 _____ have been written.
5 You need to clear some of your _____ out. They're making a mess of the house.
6 There were some beautiful pieces of _____ for sale.
7 Have you got the correct _____ for the job?
8 It's a first floor _____ and relatively cheap to rent.

WRITING TASK

> The world is unable to meet its energy needs. What three sources of renewable energy would be most effective in solving this problem in your country? Which is your preferred option?

PLAN AND WRITE A FIRST DRAFT

1 Make notes for your essay following the structure below.

- Introduction
- Point 1 (energy type 1): description/advantage(s)/disadvantage(s)
- Point 2 (energy type 2): description/advantage(s)/disadvantage(s)
- Point 3 (energy type 3): description/advantage(s)/disadvantage(s)
- Conclusion (your preferred option and why)

2 Write a first draft of your essay. Write 250–300 words.

3 Use the task checklist to review your essay for content and structure.

EDIT

TASK CHECKLIST	✔
Have you followed the five-paragraph structure above?	
Have you ranked your paragraphs in order of importance?	
Have you described each type of energy (its advantages and disadvantages) sufficiently?	
Have you written between 250–300 words?	

4 Make any necessary changes to your essay.

5 Now use the language checklist to edit your essay for language errors which are common to B2 learners.

LANGUAGE CHECKLIST	✔
Have you used appropriate subject-specific language?	
Have you spelt any energy collocations correctly?	
Have you used commas appropriately in relative clauses?	
Have you used prepositions correctly?	

6 Make any necessary changes to your essay.

OBJECTIVES REVIEW

7 Check your objectives.

I can ...

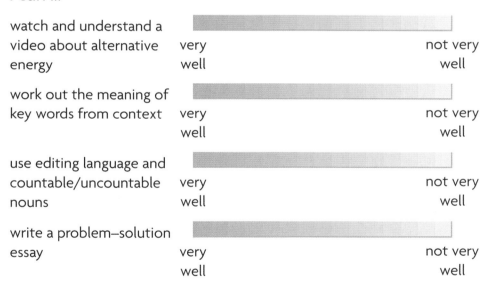

watch and understand a video about alternative energy   very well   not very well

work out the meaning of key words from context   very well   not very well

use editing language and countable/uncountable nouns   very well   not very well

write a problem–solution essay   very well   not very well

WORDLIST

UNIT VOCABULARY		ACADEMIC VOCABULARY
biofuel (n)	hydroelectricity (n)	alternative (adj)
canola oil (n)	petrol (n)	consult (v)
carbon footprint (n)	pollution (n)	consumption (n)
carbon neutral (adj)	solar power (n)	contest (v)
energy (n)	source (n)	cooperative (n)
fuel (n)	wind turbine (n)	production (n)

LEARNING OBJECTIVES

Watch and listen	Watch and understand a video about a Leonardo da Vinci design
Reading skills	Scan a text to find information
Academic writing skills	Make academic writing coherent
Writing task	Write an essay using quotations

UNL○CK YOUR KNOWLEDGE

Work with a partner. Discuss the questions below.

1 Do you like art and design? If so, what (e.g. painting, music, writing, fashion) do you like?
2 Are you artistic? If so, what kind vof artistic activities do you like doing?
3 Have you ever been to an art gallery or design show? If so, what did you see? Did you enjoy it?
4 Are art and design important for a country's economy? Why / Why not?

WATCH AND LISTEN

PREPARING TO WATCH

USING VISUALS TO PREDICT CONTENT

1 You are going to watch a video about making a Leonardo da Vinci design. Before you watch, answer the questions.

   1 What is Leonardo da Vinci famous for?

   2 Why do you think people are interested in using his 500-year-old designs?

   3 Look at the pictures from the video. What are the engineers making from da Vinci's designs?

   4 Do you think they are using traditional or modern materials and equipment?

   5 What are they going to do with the design when they have made it?

UNDERSTANDING KEY VOCABULARY

2 Match words (1–10) to definitions (a–j).

1 genius
2 sculptor
3 self-propelled
4 split
5 mechanism
6 time-consuming
7 laser
8 spring
9 cart
10 shortcut

a a piece of curved metal that can be pressed into a smaller space but then returns to its usual shape
b divide into two or more parts
c describes something that takes a lot of time to do
d able to move by its own power
e somebody who creates art from solid objects
f a quicker way of doing something in order to save time or effort
g a simple vehicle, used for carrying goods
h a part of a machine, or a set of parts that work together
i a powerful narrow beam of light that can be used as a cutting tool
j a person who has a great ability, especially in science or art

3 ▶ Watch the video and check your answers to Exercise 1.

WHILE WATCHING

4 ▶ Watch the video again and put ideas (a–h) in the order that they appear (1–8).

a The teams race their carts. _____
b One team saves time by using a laser to cut out parts. _____
c Computers are used to recreate da Vinci's design. _____
d The engineers decide to split into two teams. _____
e They wind up their springs for the first time. _____
f The teams make the wheels. _____
g One team breaks a spring. _____
h The teams notice a problem with the design. _____

5 ▶ Watch again. Are the statements below true (T) or false (F)?

1 Leonardo da Vinci had a wide range of skills. _____
2 Da Vinci's designs were typical of those being produced 500 years ago. _____
3 Da Vinci's design is very clear. _____
4 The wheels of the cart are easier to construct than the engineers expect. _____
5 Both teams use a laser cutter to make the design. _____
6 One team over-stretches both springs on their cart. _____
7 The broken spring shows that Leonardo da Vinci's design was not as good as they had thought. _____

6 Work with a partner. Discuss the questions below.

1 Was the race between the two teams fair? Why / Why not?
2 What technical advantages did the teams have over the engineers of da Vinci's time?
3 Why do you think da Vinci was interested in making a self-propelled cart? Do you think it was a good idea?

DISCUSSION

7 Work with a partner. Discuss the questions below.

1 What do you think the engineers learned from their task?
2 Leonardo also had plans for a helicopter and a parachute. Why do you think the engineers didn't try to make these designs?
3 Leonardo was an artist, scientist, mathematician, engineer, architect, musician and inventor. Why do you think it is less common for people today to be experts in more than one area?

READING 1

PREPARING TO READ

UNDERSTANDING KEY VOCABULARY

1 Match the art forms in the box to the materials or objects (1–8).

> calligraphy   pottery   sculpture   poetry   weaving   music
> furniture making   photography

1 piano, guitar, orchestra _____
2 wood and metal _____
3 clay and glaze _____
4 pen and ink _____
5 stone and bronze _____
6 words _____
7 camera _____
8 wool and thread _____

USING YOUR KNOWLEDGE TO PREDICT CONTENT

2 Read descriptions (1–4) and match the artists to the photographs of their work (a–d).

1 Andy Warhol: An artist who was famous for his prints of celebrities. _____

2 Damien Hirst: A radical British artist who famously used dead animals in his work. _____

3 Marcel Duchamp: An early twentieth-century French artist who changed what people thought of sculpture. _____

4 Frank Lloyd Wright: An American architect who focused on the role of buildings within the landscape. _____

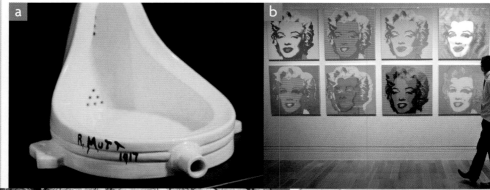

WHILE READING

Scanning to find information

Scanning is a reading technique used to look for specific information in a text. If you know what information you want from a text, you do not need to read it all. Just move your eye quickly down the page looking for the key words in the information you want. When you find it, you can just read that part in detail.

3 Scan the magazine article and put the artists in Exercise 2 in the order they appear.

SCANNING TO FIND INFORMATION

a Andy Warhol   _____

c Marcel Duchamp   _____

b Damien Hirst   _____

d Frank Lloyd Wright   _____

— Art for art's sake? —

What is art? This question has puzzled philosophers and great thinkers for centuries. A dictionary definition states that art is 'making objects, images or music, etc. that are beautiful or that express certain feelings.' This is a very broad definition. There are a number of different categories of objects and processes under the umbrella term of *art* which need to be explored.

Art is typically divided into two areas: fine art (such as painting, sculpture, music and poetry); and the applied arts (such as pottery, weaving, metal working, furniture making and calligraphy). However, some claim that the *art* label can also be attached to car design, fashion, photography, computer games, cooking, or even sport. Fine art is categorized as something which only has an aesthetic or conceptual function. This point was made over a thousand years ago by the Greek philosopher Aristotle, who wrote: 'the aim of art is to represent not the outward appearance of things but their inward significance'. He noted that artists produced objects, drama and music which reflected their emotions and ideas, rather than just trying to capture a true image of nature. Andy Warhol, the American artist famous for his Pop Art in the 1960s once said: 'an artist produces things that people don't need to have'. This is the distinction between fine and applied art. Applied arts require an object to be functional, as well as beautiful.

In the twentieth century, artists began to challenge the established notion of art. They recognized that their work belonged to the higher social classes who had the wealth to purchase art and the leisure time to enjoy it. The architect Frank Lloyd Wright commented: 'art for art's sake is a philosophy of the well-fed'. In an attempt to challenge the situation, the French painter, Marcel Duchamp submitted a toilet to an art exhibition in 1917 instead of a painting. He signed it and said: 'everything an artist produces is art'. Today, many people complain about the lack of skill in the production of conceptual artistic objects. Some contemporary artists use assistants to produce all their art for them. British artist, Damien Hirst claims that as long as he had the idea, it is his work. He has compared his art to architecture, saying: 'you have to look at it as if the artist is an architect, and we don't have a problem that great architects *don't* actually build the houses'. In fact, Hirst's mass-produced works sell for millions of dollars, and despite a hundred years of modern art, fine art is still a preserve of the wealthy.

4 Read the magazine article again. Are the statements below true (T), false (F) or the article does not say (DNS)?

1 The writer feels the dictionary definition of art is too wide. _____
2 Metal-working is an example of fine art. _____
3 Some people argue that sport is a type of art. _____
4 Aristotle was the first person to say that art should be affordable for all. _____
5 Andy Warhol invented Pop Art. _____
6 'Art for art's sake' refers to applied art. _____
7 Duchamp's toilet was sold at an art exhibition for a very high price. _____
8 Damien Hirst produces all his own art. _____

READING BETWEEN THE LINES

5 According to the article, which of the artists mentioned would probably have the opinions below? Write the initials of the artists from Exercise 3 (e.g. AW, DH, MD or FLW).

1 It is the idea of the work of art which is most important. _____
2 Art isn't functional. _____
3 Everything an artist makes can be considered art. _____
4 It does not matter if the artist doesn't actually make the work of art. _____
5 Only the rich think that art does not need a purpose. _____

DISCUSSION

6 Work with a partner. Discuss the questions below.

1 What do you think is the main purpose of art? Does it need to have a purpose, or can it just be beautiful?
2 Which of the four artists mentioned in the text do you agree with most?
3 Do you think art is only for rich people? Why / Why not?
4 Do you think activities such as car design should be classified as art?

READING 2

PREPARING TO READ

1 Work in pairs. Discuss which of the activities below you think are art.

cooking   sculpture   photography   fashion   drawing
computer games   football   gardening

2 Match adjectives (1–9) to definitions (a–i).

1	aesthetic	a	by a machine
2	mechanical	b	using new ideas
3	analogous	c	relating to beauty
4	fine	d	agree, admit something is true
5	creative	e	similar, comparable
6	objective	f	boring, uninteresting
7	acknowledge	g	suspicious, negative
8	banal	h	based on facts and reality
9	cynical	i	excellent, skilled

WHILE READING

3 Read the essay on the next page quickly. In which paragraphs (A–D) are points (1–6) discussed?

1 Fine art is a creative, collective experience. _____
2 Photography is a means of producing art. _____
3 Spending large amounts of money on equipment may result in better photographs. _____
4 Some photographers have become more vocal about calling themselves 'artists'. _____
5 The use of a camera, for example, means that photography cannot be thought of as fine art. _____
6 A list of some other types of industry that also use photography. _____

4 Match the sentences from the essay (1–5) to the corresponding paraphrase (a–e).

1 Any beauty that is perceived in the picture is the beauty of the time and place where it was taken and is not the creation of the photographer.
2 Photography is not art because it is produced with a mechanical device rather than by hand.
3 Photography is so widely used for other functions, such as police work, advertising and news reporting, that it cannot claim to be made for aesthetic purposes alone.
4 You don't take a photograph, you make it.
5 These high prices may not be enough to change people's perceptions of whether photography is art.

a Since photography is frequently used for non-artistic purposes, it cannot be considered art.
b Even if photographs are considered as valuable as paintings, people may not accept them as art.
c Art cannot be created by a machine.
d The aesthetic value of a photograph comes from the natural world, not from the skill of the person holding the camera.
e Photography requires artistic input.

Should photography be considered a fine art, like painting or sculpture?

A The production of fine art is the use of skill and imagination to create aesthetic objects or experiences which can be shared with other people. Photography is thought by some to be a form of fine art, because it is made using the same critical and creative process that a painter or sculptor would use. However, others claim that photography is not art because it is produced with a mechanical device, rather than by hand. This essay will explore both of these positions.

B Those who believe that photography is *not* a form of art present several arguments. They claim a photograph is nothing but an objective record of a particular place at a particular time. Therefore, any beauty that is perceived in the picture is the beauty of the time and place where it was taken, and is not the creation of the photographer. They also argue that sophisticated and expensive equipment often plays a greater role in the success of a photograph than the photographer's creativity. Even some of the greatest photographers acknowledge that there is a limit to the amount of influence they can have on a final product. Henri Cartier-Bresson, the famous French photographer, admitted, 'of course it's all luck'. Finally, it is often pointed out that photography is so widely used for practical functions, such as police work, advertising and news reporting, that it cannot claim to be made for aesthetic purposes alone.

C However, there are also many reasons why photography is appreciated on the same level as other recognized forms of visual art. The decisions involved in creating a photograph are analogous to those made by any other artist. A photograph is not just a banal record of the world, but a deliberately created image with its own artistic features. Ansel Adams, the American photographer, commented on this point when he noted: 'You don't take a photograph, you *make* it.' There is a growing trend for photographers to call themselves artists. Cynical observers say this is because artists can sell their pieces in the higher-priced fine-art markets, whereas photographers cannot. A photograph by German artist Andreas Gursky, for example, recently sold for almost four and a half million dollars. However, these high prices may not be enough to change people's perceptions of whether photography is art.

D The arguments about whether photography is art have been discussed since the earliest cameras were used. The creative process involved in taking a fine photograph, deciding what, when and how the picture should be taken, is certainly similar to the process of making fine art. However, cameras are also increasingly used to take photographs for non-artistic functions. Although we cannot say that photography itself is necessarily art, we can certainly see that it is a medium that can be *used* to make art.

READING BETWEEN THE LINES

5 Match opinions (1–6) with people (a–f).

1 There's no reason for a great photograph to be any cheaper than a great painting.
2 Even a child could take a great picture of that view.
3 There's a lot more skill to making a picture than just pointing a camera at something and clicking. It's something that I create.
4 Most of us would just walk by and not notice something that could make a fabulous photo. And even if we did notice we probably wouldn't know how to take a photo that would stir other people's feelings.
5 It all depends what the camera is used for.
6 Sometimes you just see something that will make a great picture and the light is perfect and you have your camera with you. At other times, nothing seems to be right.

a Ansel Adams
b Henri Cartier-Bresson
c Andreas Gursky
d The author of the essay
e Somebody who believes photography is art
f Somebody who doesn't believe photography is art

DISCUSSION

6 Work with a partner. Discuss the questions below.

1 Do you like taking photographs? Why / Why not? If so, what kinds of photographs do you like taking?
2 Should photography be considered an art form? If so, is it fine art or applied art?
3 Is photography less of an art form now we can digitally improve our photographs?
4 Can a photograph really be worth $4.5 million? Why / Why not?

⊙ LANGUAGE DEVELOPMENT

EXPLANATION

Quotations and reporting information

In academic writing, we often refer to what somebody else has written to support our arguments. There are two ways to do this.

Quotations use direct speech – repeating the writer's exact words.

> Henri Cartier-Bresson said, 'Of course it's all luck.'

Paraphrasing uses reported speech – explaining the opinion without using the same words.

> Henri Cartier-Bresson admitted that luck was the most important factor.

Quotations

When using quotations in a text, introduce them using a relevant verb. Two common verbs for this are *state* and *say*.

> A dictionary definition **states** that art is 'making objects, images or music, etc. that are beautiful or that express feelings'.
> Andy Warhol … **said**: 'An artist produces things that people don't need to have'.

State and *say* are neutral verbs – they do not show how strongly you think the author (or person you are quoting) feels about the statement.

Some verbs, however, can be used to show how strongly you think the original author feels. For example, *argue*, *insist* and *deny* show that the author was very sure about what he or she said, whereas *suggest* and *imply* show the author was less sure.

1 Read quotations (1–4) and complete the paraphrases below with a strong or weak verb from the Explanation box. Put the verb in the correct form.

1 'It is absolutely essential that children study art at school.' (Head Teacher)
The Head Teacher _____ that art should be part of the curriculum.

2 'Perhaps the statue could be put in the main square.' (Sculptor)
The sculptor _____ that the main square would be a suitable location for the statue.

3 'We cannot say art is only for the wealthy because many great artists never knew anything but poverty throughout their lives.' (Lecturer)
The lecturer _____ that it was not unusual for famous artists to live in poverty.

4 'I told you. I did not steal the painting.' (Burglar)
The burglar _____ that he had stolen the painting.

2 Read the quotations below and write sentences quoting some of the author's words. Look at the punctuation in the example and check your sentences.

'A picture is worth a thousand words.' (Napoleon Bonaparte)
Napoleon Bonaparte explained that every picture could tell us the same amount as 'a thousand words'.
1 'A picture is a poem without words.' (Horace)
2 'Don't think. Thinking is the enemy of creativity.' (Ray Bradbury)
3 'Creativity takes courage.' (Henri Matisse)

3 Read the quotations below and paraphrase them (do not quote directly).

'A picture is worth a thousand words.' (Napoleon Bonaparte)
Napoleon Bonaparte felt that images expressed ideas more directly than writing.
1 'Creativity involves breaking out of established patterns in order to look at things in a different way.' (Edward de Bono)
2 'Clean out a corner of your mind and creativity will instantly fill it.' (Dee Hock)
3 'Creativity is allowing yourself to make mistakes.' (Scott Adams)

DESCRIBING ART

4 Match adjectives (1–8) to definitions (a–h).

1 abstract   a causes strong feelings of sadness or sympathy
2 expressive   b showing people or things in a similar way to real life
3 decorative   c relating to ideas, not to real things
4 figurative   d made to look attractive
5 moving   e showing what somebody thinks or feels
6 avant-garde   f very big
7 lifelike   g ideas and styles that are very original and modern
8 monumental   h looks very real

5 Complete the sentences with the adjectives from Exercise 3.
1 The _____ bronze sculpture weighs seven tonnes.
2 It was a _____ performance which left many people in tears.
3 I think art is purely _____ . It is only there to look nice.
4 The sculpture was so _____ people were a little scared by it.
5 Her work was _____ and her ideas did not become popular until after her death.
6 _____ art can look easy to produce, because there are no figurative images.
7 He was interested in _____ art and produced many lifelike portraits.
8 The paint was applied quickly to the picture in an _____ and emotional way.

CRITICAL THINKING

At the end of this unit, you will write an essay using quotations. Look at this unit's writing task in the box below.

> Fashion, cooking, video games and sport have all been likened to fine art. Choose *one* of these and discuss whether it should be considered fine art, comparable to painting or sculpture.

UNDERSTAND

1 Read quotations (1–8) and decide whether they support or challenge the idea that fashion, cooking, video games or sport can be fine art.

	support	challenge
1 'Unlike art, fashion rarely expresses more than the headlines of history.' Alice Rawsthorn		
2 'Some say football is a matter of life and death – I'd say it's much more important than that.' Bill Shankly		
3 'Competition, it might be said, is the game's most fundamental principle, and it's precisely what distinguishes art from sport.' Steve Reynolds		
4 'Video games are a unique form of artistic expression through what I call the "three voices": the voice of the designer or artist, the voice of the game and its mechanics, and the voice of the player.' Chris Melissinos		
5 'The same amount of artistic expression goes into clothes, a piece of pottery or a painting.' Zandra Rhodes		
6 'For most gamers, video games represent a loss of those precious hours we have available to make ourselves more cultured, civilized and empathetic.' Roger Ebert		
7 Cooking 'doesn't involve the sense of the transmission of human emotion in the way that the arts at their highest do.' Denis Dutton		
8 'The art of cooking: it's when you mix craftsmanship at the highest level with creativity.' Eric Ripert		

2 Work with a partner. Discuss which quotations you agree with and why.

3 Complete the sentences. Give reasons for your answers.

1 I ~~agree~~ / disagree with Zandra Rhodes who argues that 'the same amount of artistic expression goes into clothes, a piece of pottery or a painting' because *clothes have to be practical enough to wear.*

2 I *agree / disagree* with Eric Ripert when he says cooking is the mixture of 'craftsmanship at the highest level with creativity' because ...

3 I *agree / disagree* with Steve Reynolds who wrote that the element of competition in football is 'precisely what distinguishes art from sport' because ...

4 I *agree / disagree* with Roger Ebert that 'video games represent a loss of those precious hours we have available to make ourselves more cultured, civilized and empathetic' because ...

WRITING

GRAMMAR FOR WRITING

EXPLANATION

Substitution

In academic writing, we try to avoid repetition when possible. To do this, we can substitute pronouns or other words for nouns or noun phrases.

In the sentence below, *this* is used to avoid repetition.

Although many people find cars beautiful, ~~finding cars beautiful~~ this does not make cars art.

1 Read the paragraph below and underline the words the author has substituted for the full name of the car.

The Jaguar E-type is probably one of the most famous cars ever produced. The two-seater roadster was the fastest production sports car on the market in 1961. It was designed to be an expressive mixture of a racing car and something you could use every day. The aerodynamic styling of the car is functional yet beautiful. The bullet shape of the E-type contrasts with the body's curves. The machine's most prominent feature is the long, projecting bonnet which contains the powerful engine. The view of the car's shape is as beautiful from the driving seat as it is to the pedestrian. It is easy to see why Enzo Ferrari called it 'the most beautiful car in the world'.

Ellipsis

Another way to avoid repetition is to leave out some words which have already been mentioned. This is called ellipsis.

Some photographs have a clear meaning but other photographs **do not** ~~have a clear meaning~~.

2 Read the paragraph below and delete any words or phrases which can be removed without affecting the meaning of the text. Add any substitutions (such as pronouns) which you think are necessary.

The Scream is the popular name given to each of four paintings of *The Scream* by the artist Edvard Munch who painted *The Scream* between 1893 and 1910. The pictures of *The Scream* show a figure against a landscape with a red sky. The National Gallery, Oslo, holds one painting of *The Scream*, the Munch Museum holds two more paintings of *The Scream* and the fourth version of *The Scream* sold for $119m at Sotheby's on 2 May 2012. To explain the picture of *The Scream*, the artist Edvard Munch wrote in his diary: 'One evening I felt tired and ill. I stopped and looked out over the sea – the sun was setting, and the clouds were turning blood red. I sensed a scream passing through nature; it seemed to me that I heard the scream.'

ACADEMIC WRITING SKILLS

Coherence

When writing, it is important to show the relationship between different parts of the text. This is called coherence and it will make your writing easier for the reader to follow. Some words we use to make our writing coherent are:

Pronouns: *they, them, it, one*, etc.
Conjunctions and connectors: *however, therefore, in contrast, although*, etc.
Determiners: *this, that, these, those*, etc.
Linking phrases: *for example, in the same way*, etc.

1 Read the paragraph below and complete the text with the words in the box.

> they (x2)   because   in the same way   them   objects   although

(1)_____ some people argue that cars are art (2)_____ they are beautiful, (3)_____ are still primarily functional rather than beautiful. To many people, cars are just vehicles which transport (4)_____ and their goods from one place to another. (5)_____ see them as useful tools (6)_____ as knives, chairs or mobile phones. These are all mass-produced (7)_____ , so cannot be seen as art.

2 Read sentences (1–6) and write a coherent paragraph using all the information. Use Exercise 1 to help you.

1 In some cases, there are similarities between cars and fine art.
2 Some classic cars are as rare and as expensive as fine art.
3 A 1962 Ferrari GTO (a classic car) made $35 million in a sale in 2012.
4 Classic cars are not always a practical means of transport.
5 According to some, classic cars have a personality.
6 Some people describe their feelings towards their classic car as 'love'.

WRITING TASK

Fashion, cooking, video games and sport have all been likened to fine art. Choose *one* of these and discuss whether it should be considered fine art, comparable to painting or sculpture.

1 Make notes using the essay plan below.

PLAN AND WRITE
A FIRST DRAFT

Introduction
Body paragraph 1
• Evidence in favour of one position (i.e. agree or disagree)
• Use of quotation(s) to support this position
Body paragraph 2
• Evidence in favour of the other position (i.e. agree or disagree)
• Use of quotation(s) to support this position
Conclusion
• Statement of your position (either agree, disagree or a mixture of the two)

2 Write your essay. Use your essay plan to help you structure your ideas. Write 250–300 words.

3 Use the task checklist to review your essay for content and structure.

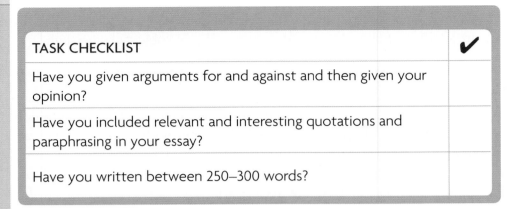

TASK CHECKLIST	✔
Have you given arguments for and against and then given your opinion?	
Have you included relevant and interesting quotations and paraphrasing in your essay?	
Have you written between 250–300 words?	

4 Make any necessary changes to your essay.

5 Now use the language checklist to edit your essay for language errors which are common to B2 learners.

LANGUAGE CHECKLIST	✔
Have you used a range of structures to make your text coherent?	
Have you used substitution and ellipsis in your essay where appropriate?	
Have you introduced quotations and paraphrasing appropriately?	
Have you used a range of adjectives to describe art and spelt them correctly?	

6 Make any necessary changes to your essay.

OBJECTIVES REVIEW

7 Check your objectives.

I can ...

watch and understand a
video about a Leonardo
da Vinci design

very   not very
well   well

scan a text to find
information

very   not very
well   well

make academic writing
coherent

very   not very
well   well

write an essay using
quotations

very   not very
well   well

WORDLIST

UNIT VOCABULARY			ACADEMIC VOCABULARY
abstract (adj)	laser (n)	sculpture (n)	claim (v)
aesthetic (adj)	lifelike (adj)	self-propelled (adj)	describe (v)
avant-garde (adj)	mechanical (adj)	shortcut (n)	discuss (v)
banal (adj)	mechanism (n)	specific (adj)	established (adj)
calligraphy (n)	monumental (adj)	split (v)	illustrate (v)
cart (n)	moving (adj)	spring (n)	prove (v)
creative (adj)	objective (adj)	time-consuming (adj)	
decorative (adj)	poetry (n)	weaving (n)	
figurative (adj)	pottery (n)		
genius (n)	sculptor (n)		

LEARNING OBJECTIVES

Watch and listen	Watch and understand a video about the Khanty of Siberia
Reading skills	Use your knowledge to predict content
Academic writing skills	Interpret and predict trends from a population pyramid
Writing task	Describe population data and its implications

UNLOCK YOUR KNOWLEDGE

1 Are elderly people generally respected in your culture?
   Why? / Why not?

2 How is respect or disrespect shown to elderly people in your culture?

3 How has everyday life changed in the past 50 years for people who
   are now elderly?

WATCH AND LISTEN

PREPARING TO WATCH

UNDERSTANDING
KEY VOCABULARY

1 Match definitions (1–7) to the words in the box.

> pen   reindeer   threaten   round up   wander   inspire   ancestor

1 To bring together people or animals
2 A person related to you who lived a long time ago
3 A type of deer with large horns
4 To go from place to place
5 To put at risk
6 A small area surrounded by a fence for keeping animals in
7 To make someone feel that they want to do something and can do it

2 Complete the sentences below with the correct form of the words from Exercise 1.

1 _____ are able to live in the freezing temperatures of the Arctic.
2 He discovered that one of his _____ was a prince.
3 Globalization _____ traditional ways of life around the world.
4 The animals are kept in a _____ at night.
5 Cowboys in the west of the USA used to _____ wild cattle.
6 Nomadic peoples have always _____ the earth in search of food and water.
7 Watching that Russian film _____ me to go to Moscow.

USING YOUR
KNOWLEDGE TO
PREDICT CONTENT

3 Work in pairs. You are going to watch a video about Alexei and Dulcia Moldanov, who are members of the Khanty tribe in Russia. Guess whether the statements below are true (T) or false (F).

1 The tribe live in a hot country. _____
2 They live in the city. _____
3 They work with animals. _____
4 Their traditions are in danger. _____
5 The video is about two generations of a family. _____
6 Life is hard for the elderly tribespeople. _____

4 ▶ Watch the video and check your predictions.

WHILE WATCHING

5 ▶ Watch the video again. Number the ideas below in the order that they appear (1–7).

UNDERSTANDING
MAIN IDEAS

a Siberia is known for its long, freezing winters.   _____
b The Russian Federation is an enormous country.   _____
c The Moldanovs' son, Misha, helps with the reindeer.   _____
d The traditional way of life of the Khanty is threatened.   _____
e Perhaps Misha's son, Daniil, will want to protect the Khanty
   way of life.   _____
f The Moldanovs are members of the Khanty tribe of Siberia.   _____
g The Moldanovs are elderly and need help with the reindeer.   _____

6 ▶ Watch again. Complete the sentences below with a number from the box. You do not need to use all the numbers.

LISTENING FOR
DETAIL

> 28,000   200 (x2)   11   2,000   7   2,800

1 The Russian Federation contains _____ time zones.
2 Temperatures in Siberia are below freezing for up to _____ months of the year.
3 There are _____ Khanty people living in Siberia today.
4 The Moldanovs keep _____ reindeer.
5 Misha lives _____ miles away from his parents.

DISCUSSION

7 Work with a partner. Discuss the questions below.

1 Do countries have a responsibility to protect the traditional way of life of their indigenous people?
2 Are there any indigenous people in your country whose way of life is threatened?
3 What kinds of help do people in your country give their elderly parents?
4 Whose responsibility is it to look after elderly people? The family or the state?

READING 1

PREPARING TO READ

USING YOUR
KNOWLEDGE TO
PREDICT CONTENT

Predicting

Before you read a text, it is useful to look at the title and introduction (if there is one) and think what you already know about the subject. It may help you to understand difficult parts of the text.

You now have some knowledge of the Khanty tribe from the video. You know that they live in Siberia, they keep reindeer and live without gas or electricity. So, if you read an article called *How the Khanty Survive Winter*, you can make some guesses about unknown words.

For example, if the text says *On feast days, they kill young cattle for venison*, you can try to guess what *venison* is. You know that the Khanty keep reindeer, so *venison* is probably the meat from young reindeer.

1 You are going to read an interview called *The Social and Economic Impact of Ageing*. Use your knowledge to write three facts that might be in the interview.

1 _____ 2 _____ 3 _____

2 Try to predict the answers to the questions below.

1 Has healthcare throughout the world improved over the last 50 years?
2 Are people living longer or dying earlier?
3 What kind of problems might old people face?
4 What kind of problems might a society face if it has more elderly people?
5 What kind of benefits can an older population bring to society?

3 Read the interview to check your ideas. If your ideas were different, why do you think that is?

WHILE READING

READING FOR DETAIL

4 Read the interview again. Are the statements below true (T), false (F) or the article does not say (DNS)?

1 Robert Huffenheimer teaches at Oxford University. _____
2 The average age of the world's population has increased significantly over the last 50 years. _____
3 Most older people have relatives nearby. _____
4 There are both benefits and disadvantages to an ageing population. _____
5 So far, private companies have ignored these demographic changes. _____
6 Countries with an older population have higher education costs. _____
7 On average, older people spend four hours per day online. _____
8 Countries can benefit from the skills of older people. _____

THE SOCIAL AND ECONOMIC IMPACT OF AGEING

In the next instalment of our series on demographic changes, we interview Professor Robert Huffenheimer, an expert on the phenomenon of ageing.

What exactly does ageing mean?

It means the population in many countries is, on average, getting older. Incredibly, between 1955 and 2010, average life expectancy in wealthier countries increased by nearly half, from 48 to 67 years, worldwide.

What impact is this ageing process likely to have globally?

Well, obviously it is a good thing that people are living longer, but as a result of these changes there are a number of issues which have to be dealt with.

For example?

In certain countries, an increasing number of older people are living by themselves, often without any relatives living nearby. Some older people are simply unable to look after themselves, and others can only do so if their houses are specially adapted. Likewise, they may be unable to go shopping or wash themselves, and so they need someone, perhaps a professional, to help. And, of course, older people do need social activities as well.

And how are societies adapting to this?

Supermarkets, for example, have introduced more home-delivery services, which have been particularly beneficial for older people. In addition, there has been significant growth in companies providing services which would traditionally have been undertaken by relatives. This includes private nursing care and the 'meals on wheels' service, which delivers food to your door.

Are there any other areas where the impact of ageing can be clearly seen?

Although it is not a problem yet, many governments are worried about the economic impact of an ageing population. With fewer people working and paying taxes, it is obvious that governments will have less money to pay for things like health and education.

What advantages can an older population bring?

In countries where the percentage of children is lower, there are fewer education costs. In more developed countries, older people tend to have more savings and more free time. They might spend time online, or travel, or even go back to education. Of course, older people do have a lot of experience, and if they can, some continue working in a voluntary capacity. This adds a lot to society.

5 Complete the sentences with no more than three words from the interview.

1 Specially adapted houses help elderly people who can't _____ _____ _____ .

2 Older people require _____ _____ as well as professional help with shopping and washing.

3 Home deliveries and _____ _____ _____ are commercial services provided for the elderly.

4 Governments are concerned by the _____ _____ of a large number of elderly people in the population.

5 Older people are free to travel and learn new skills because they have more _____ and _____ _____ .

6 Experienced older people may choose to do _____ work to help society.

READING BETWEEN THE LINES

MAKING INFERENCES FROM THE TEXT

6 Work with a partner. Discuss reasons for the things below.

1 Life expectancy increases dramatically.
2 Old people are living further away from their relatives.
3 Supermarkets have started selling online.
4 Older people tend to have more savings.
5 Older people want to go back to education.

DISCUSSION

7 Work with a partner. Discuss the questions below.

1 Does your country have a young or an ageing population?
2 What problems do elderly people in your community face?
3 What do you think can be done to ensure that elderly people in society are protected and cared for?

READING 2

PREPARING TO READ

1 Work in pairs. Some countries have a higher percentage of young people than older people. Discuss the problems, impact and solutions there might be with this.

2 Read sentences (1–4) and choose the correct definitions (a, b or c) for the words in bold.

1 The population pyramid for Saudi Arabia is **bottom heavy**.
  a a greater percentage towards the higher end of something
  b balanced, in equal proportion
  c a higher percentage towards the lower end of something
2 The **median age** is just 22.
  a when people are considered to be 'middle-aged'
  b the age at which 50% of the population is older and 50% is younger
  c the age when people legally become adults
3 This 'youth **bulge**' is likely to have a huge impact.
  a small increase   b large increase   c sharp decrease
4 There is likely to be a higher demand for housing than **supply**.
  a the amount which is available
  b the amount which is desired
  c the amount which people can afford

WHILE READING

3 Read the essay on the next page about the effects of a young population on a society. Check your ideas from Exercise 1.

4 Complete each sentence with a word or number.

1 Saudi Arabia has a very _____ population.
2 More than one in _____ of the population is aged between 0 and 9.
3 _____ % of the population is under 30.
4 Almost _____ % of Saudi Arabia's population is between 30 and 39.
5 The proportion of Saudis under 40 is _____ than the proportion of under-40s in the whole Middle Eastern region.
6 Saudi Arabia is number _____ in the world for government spending on education, as a proportion of its GDP.
7 There is a lack of employment in both the public and private _____ .
8 A city that is between the mountains and the sea has limited space for _____ .

What are the effects of a young population on a society?

1   There is a well-documented problem with the ageing of the global population, but there are also areas of the world where demographics are very different. In many parts of the Middle East and North Africa, there is a much higher proportion of young people. This essay will explore the demographic profile of one such country, Saudi Arabia, and the effects this has on the country's society and economics.

2   The diagram shows the proportion of men and women in Saudi Arabia and their age ranges in 2010. The population pyramid is certainly very bottom heavy, showing clearly that the Kingdom has a much younger population than average. Upon close analysis, it can be seen that over 21% of the population is under the age of ten, and approximately 36% of the total population is aged between 10 and 29. The number of Saudis in their 30s is particularly high, with almost one in five of the total population falling within this ten-year age range. Over three-quarters of the Saudi population is under 40, compared to the global figure for under-40s, which is 67%. However, Saudi Arabia is typical of the Middle East as a whole, where 65% of the region's population is under the age of 40. In Saudi Arabia, the median age is just 22.

3   This 'youth bulge' is having a huge impact in a number of different areas, such as education, housing and the economy. The high percentage of children and young people means that Saudi Arabia's education costs are high. Indeed, it spends more of its GDP (around 9.6%) on education than any other country in the world. The government is leading a university expansion programme to cope with the number of students moving through the school system every year.

4   This 'youth bulge' also has an impact on employment opportunities for young people. Unless Saudi Arabia's public sector can employ enough people or attract more private sector employers, more expenditure will be needed on unemployment benefits.

5   There is a similar challenge in terms of housing, with more demand than supply. This is a particular problem in cities, such as Jeddah, where outward expansion is geographically impossible. As a consequence, houses become more expensive and young people may be unable to buy their own home.

6   Although Saudi Arabia faces several challenges in terms of education, employment and housing as a result of its young population, it does not have to cope with the demands of an ageing population. Healthcare and pension costs are lower, allowing more funds to be allocated to improving the lives of young people.

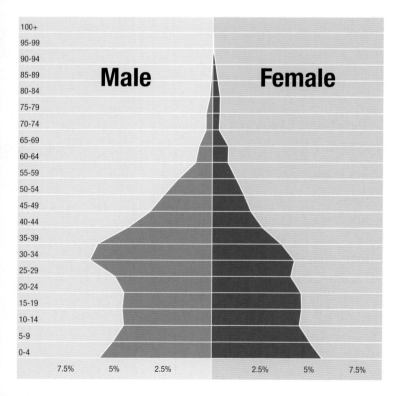

READING BETWEEN THE LINES

5 Work with a partner. Find the words and phrases below in the essay and discuss what they mean.

WORKING OUT
MEANING FROM
CONTEXT

1 well-documented
2 demographic profile
3 upon close analysis
4 GDP

5 challenge
6 as a consequence
7 funds to be allocated to

DISCUSSION

6 Work with a partner. Discuss the questions below.

1 What are the advantages to a country of having a younger population?
2 In a country with public taxation, why is it good to have more workers than pensioners?
3 Should governments raise the retirement age to reduce the amount paid out in pensions?

⊙ LANGUAGE DEVELOPMENT

RETIREMENT AND THE ELDERLY VOCABULARY

1 Match the nouns in the box to the correct group of words (1–6) to make collocations and phrases.

> pension   years   retirement   age   health   memory

compulsory be close to early active	1 _____	plan age	old advanced pension retirement	4 _____	-related discrimination
draw a contribute to a pay into a a private a state	2 _____	scheme	a good short-term childhood happy bring back a	5 _____	loss
in perfect ill	3 _____	care centre worker problem	recent coming later early	6 _____	of marriage ago

2 Complete the sentences with phrases from Exercise 1.

1 Many people want to continue working when they reach

    _____ .

2 In 40 _____ , they never had an argument.

3 Many companies _____ scheme,
   in addition to paying a salary.

4 We wish you a long and _____ .

5 He had to retire due to _____ .

6 My grandfather has _____ and tells
   fascinating stories from his childhood.

7 In _____ , the average retirement
   age of the population is likely to rise.

8 A _____ comes in every day to
   change his bandages.

9 When you reach _____ , you can
   often get discounts on educational courses.

ACADEMIC COLLOCATIONS WITH PREPOSITIONS

3 Complete the phrases and phrasal verbs with the correct prepositions
(*in, on, with, up, of*).

1 _____ brief   5 identify _____

2 range _____   6 _____ theory

3 focus _____   7 rely _____

4 sum _____   8 _____ contrast

4 Complete the sentences below with the correct phrases and phrasal
verbs from Exercise 3.

1 States may encounter financial challenges when an increasing number
   of older people have to _____ them for support.

2 States with a younger population have high education costs.
   _____ , those with an older population have to spend more on
   health care.

3 There is a _____ voluntary work opportunities for pensioners,
   such as sports coaching, business mentoring, gardening and counselling.

4 There is a tendency to _____ the problems faced by the
   elderly, not their valuable contribution to society.

5 _____ , the major problem an ageing population will face is
   how to fund healthcare.

6 While many strategies may seem to work _____ , in practice
   they rarely succeed.

7 Society has problems when its older citizens cannot _____
   its younger members.

8 To _____ , this report's key recommendation is that more
   educational opportunities should be provided for the over-60s.

CRITICAL THINKING

1 Look at the population graph for Japan and answer the questions.

1 How old is the data in the diagram?
2 What is the total population of Japan?
3 Are there more over-40s or under-40s in Japan?
4 On average, do Japanese men or women live longer?
5 Approximately what percentage of the population is aged over 60?
6 How is the graph different from the one for Saudi Arabia in Reading 2? What are the reasons for this?

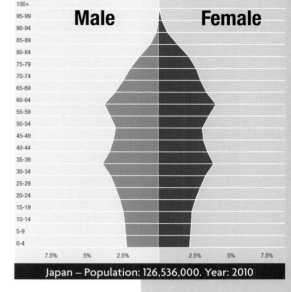

Japan – Population: 126,536,000. Year: 2010

2 Look at the two graphs below. They are predictions for the year 2050. Which do you think relates to Japan, and which to Saudi Arabia? Why?

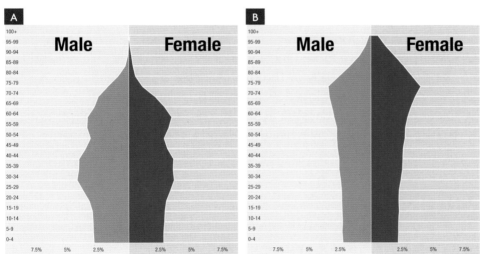

3 Identify the possible problems from the list below for a society with an elderly population.

1 youth unemployment
2 housing shortage
3 high pension costs
4 increased healthcare costs
5 stress on the education system
6 lower consumer spending
7 declining fertility
8 higher taxes
9 increased emigration
10 increased immigration

4 Write a phrase from Exercise 3 in each sentence.

1 _____ are likely to occur because more elderly people will require hospital treatment and help with ill health.

2 If people work for longer and retire at an older age, _____ may result.

3 _____ may be required because there are fewer people of working age paying tax on their income.

4 Unless the age at which people have to retire increases, there will be _____ which the taxes will need to pay for.

5 As the population ages, there are fewer people having children. This _____ means that the population will actually decrease.

6 In order to replace the lost workforce and to increase levels of taxation, _____ may be adopted as a government policy.

5 Work in pairs. Look at the statements below. Which advantage of an older population do you think is the most important?

1 Older people have a great deal of knowledge and experience which are valuable in the workplace.

2 Older people have more time and money to help their children and grandchildren financially or through childcare and domestic jobs.

3 Older societies result in a slower global population growth.

4 Older people these days are active and productive. Many have savings to help pay for their own healthcare and a comfortable standard of living.

WRITING

GRAMMAR FOR WRITING

Numerical words and phrases

It is important to simplify complex statistical information when writing a description of a graph or chart. To do this, we can use generalizations to introduce the data and specific examples to give details or justify a claim. Numerical words and phrases help us do this.

1 Look at the pie chart and complete the sentences (1–8) with words from the box.

Population by age

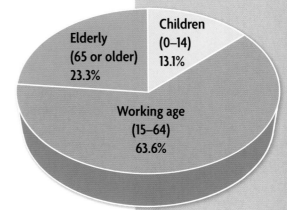

> majority   double   minority   quarter   half
> times   proportion   triple

1 The overwhelming _____ of Japanese people are of working age.
2 A sizable _____ (23%) are over 65 years old.
3 The number of Japanese people who are of working age is almost five _____ more than those under 14.
4 A significant _____ of the Japanese population are of working age.
5 The percentage of people aged 65 and older is nearly _____ the percentage of children.
6 The percentage of the population who are of working age is nearly _____ those who are pensioners.
7 More than _____ the population is of working age.
8 Just under a _____ of the population is over 65.

Language of prediction

When we describe a graph, we sometimes predict what might happen in the future based on the trends in the graph. We can use a number of different ways to show that a statement is a prediction.

2 Match the sentence halves.

1 There is likely
2 There may
3 The number of
4 The population is set
5 We are unlikely to
6 Unemployment is
7 Food prices

a well be more wealthy people with time on their hands.
b to be more competition for places at care homes in the future.
c projected to increase in the coming years.
d to rise sharply during the next few years.
e young people is expected to remain the same for the foreseeable future.
f are predicted to come down.
g see a sharp rise in immigration based on current trends.

3 Write sentences with the same meaning. Include the word in brackets. More than one answer is possible.

1 The population will increase in the future.

_____ (likely)

2 Oil prices will come down this year.

_____ (may well)

3 Unemployment will remain at the same level in the coming months.

_____ (predicted)

4 The cost of living will rise over the decade.

_____ (set)

5 There will be more competition for university places in the future.

_____ (expected)

6 There will not be a reduction in the number of schools.

_____ (unlikely)

7 Salaries will rise because of access to better training and education.

_____ (projected)

ACADEMIC WRITING SKILLS

INTERPRETING GRAPHS AND CHARTS

1 Look at the example writing task. Are statements (1–8) true (T) or false (F)?

The diagram below shows the global population by age in 1950 and 2000 and the projected figures for 2050. Write an essay describing the information and suggesting what the potential global impact could be if the 2050 projections are correct.

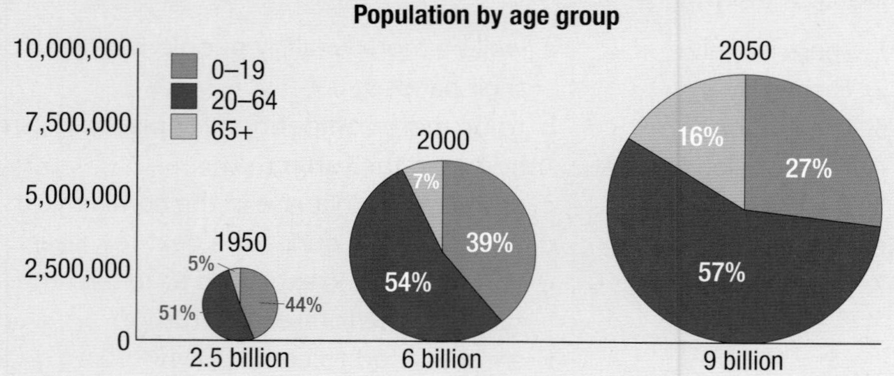

Population by age group

1 You should mention all the data in the diagram. _____
2 You do not have to mention exact numbers. _____
3 You should start your essay by copying the title or the caption. _____
4 You should compare the charts. _____
5 You should talk about general trends over time. _____
6 You do not need an introduction or conclusion in this type of essay. _____
7 Your writing does not need to be formal in this type of essay. _____
8 You should give your own ideas. _____

2 Which of the following sentences would you include when writing the essay in Exercise 1? Give reasons for your answers.

1 In 1950, there were 44% 0–19-year-olds, 51% 20–64-year-olds and 5% 65+ year-olds.

2 I think it'll be really tough to be a teenager in 2050 cos there'll be a lot of old people.

3 Although there was only a 2% rise in the number of over-65s between 1950 and 2000, this figure is projected to rise by nearly 10% by 2050.

4 This essay will describe the global population by age in 1950 and 2000 and the projected figures for 2050.

5 The predicted decrease in the number of young people is likely to have a range of social and economic effects.

WRITING TASK

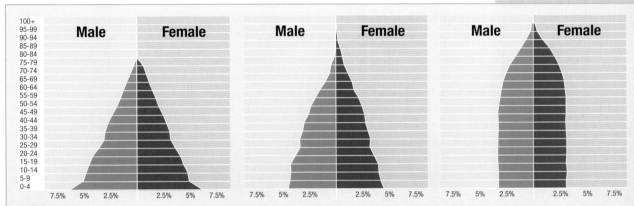

The population pyramids above show the global population by age in 1950 and 2010 and the projected figures for 2100. Write an essay describing the information and suggesting what the potential global impact could be if the 2100 projections are correct.

1 Look again at the structure of the essay in Reading 2 on page 184. Write the paragraph numbers of Reading 2 next to the purposes below.

PLAN AND WRITE
A FIRST DRAFT

  a Presentation and description of the data from the graphs   _____

  b Second most important implication   _____

  c Most important implication   _____

  d General overview of the impact of this data   _____

  e Third most important implication   _____

  f Introduction   _____

2 Look at the population pyramids above. Write one sentence about what they represent. Paraphrase the language in the writing task.

_____

_____

3 Choose three aspects of the data to write about. Consider points that show the general picture or overall trends of the pyramids.

Point 1: _____

Point 2: _____

Point 3: _____

4 Summarize the most interesting or noticeable trend in one sentence.

Main trend: _____

5 Think of three important implications of your main argument. A model for Reading 2 is given below as an example.

> **Reading 2:** Saudi Arabia
>
> **Main trend:** Saudi Arabia is experiencing a 'youth bulge'.
>
> **Implication 1:** effect on education
>
> **Implication 2:** effect on the economy
>
> **Implication 3:** effect on housing

6 Using the paragraph structure given in Exercise 1 and your notes in Exercises 2–5, write the first draft of your essay. Write 250–300 words.

7 Use the task checklist to review your essay for content and structure.

TASK CHECKLIST	✔
Does the structure of your essay follow the structure in Reading 2?	
Have you talked about both the data and its implications?	
Do your examples back up your main trend and its implications?	
Have you written between 250–300 words?	

8 Make any necessary changes to your essay.

9 Now use the language checklist to edit your essay for language errors which are common to B2 learners.

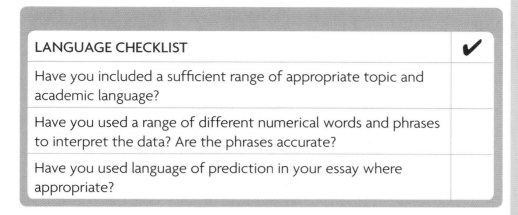

LANGUAGE CHECKLIST	✔
Have you included a sufficient range of appropriate topic and academic language?	
Have you used a range of different numerical words and phrases to interpret the data? Are the phrases accurate?	
Have you used language of prediction in your essay where appropriate?	

10 Make any necessary changes to your essay.

OBJECTIVES REVIEW

11 Check your objectives.

I can …

watch and understand a video about the Khanty of Siberia	very well	not very well
use my knowledge to predict content	very well	not very well
interpret and predict trends from a population pyramid	very well	not very well
describe population data and its implications	very well	not very well

WORDLIST

UNIT VOCABULARY		ACADEMIC VOCABULARY	
demographic (n and adj)	retirement (n)	decline (v)	in theory (ph)
economic impact (n)	shortage (n)	focus on (v)	protect (v)
elderly (adj)	social activities (n)	identify with (v)	range of (ph)
healthcare (n)	unemployment (n)	in brief (ph)	rely on (v)
pension (n)	workforce (n)	in contrast (ph)	sum up (v)

GLOSSARY

Vocabulary	Pronunciation	Part of speech	Definition
UNIT 1			
at the moment	/ət ðə ˈməʊmənt/	(ph)	now
at the present time	/ət ðə ˈprezənt taɪm/	(ph)	now
authenticity	/ɔːθenˈtɪsəti/	(n)	the quality of being real or true
chef	/ʃef/	(n)	a skilled and trained cook who works in a hotel or restaurant, especially the most important cook
confuse	/kənˈfjuːz/	(v)	to make someone unable to think clearly, or to make something difficult to understand
consumption	/kənˈsʌmpʃən/	(n)	the amount of something that someone uses, eats, or drinks
continue	/kənˈtɪnjuː/	(v)	to keep happening, existing or doing something
cooking equipment	/ˈkʊkɪŋ ɪˈkwɪpmənt/	(n)	the set of necessary tools for a particular purpose
currently	/ˈkʌrəntli/	(v)	at the present time
diet	/daɪət/	(n)	the type of food that someone usually eats
discount	/dɪˈskaʊnt/	(n)	a reduction in price
ethnic group	/ˈeθnɪk gruːp/	(n)	a group of people with a particular race or nationality
exclude	/ɪksˈkluːd/	(v)	to not allow someone or something to take part in an activity or enter a place
exhaust	/ɪgˈzɔːst/	(v)	to use something completely
food miles	/fuːd maɪlz/	(n)	the distance between the place where food is grown or made and the place where it is eaten
formerly	/ˈfɔːməli/	(adv)	in the past
freshness	/ˈfreʃnɪs/	(n)	the state of being recently made, done or arrived, and not yet changed by time
goods	/gʊdz/	(n)	things for sale
historically	/hɪˈstɒrɪkli/	(adv)	in a way that is connected to history
increase	/ɪnˈkriːs/	(v)	to get bigger or to make something bigger in amount or size
increase	/ˈɪnkriːs/	(n)	a rise in the amount or size of something
industrialize	/ɪnˈdʌstriəlaɪz/	(v)	to develop industry
ingredient	/ɪnˈgriːdiənt/	(n)	a food that is used with other foods in the preparation of a particular dish
insist	/ɪnˈsɪst/	(v)	to demand that something must be done or that you must have a particular thing
IT communication	/aɪˈtiː kəmjuːnɪˈkeɪʃən/	(n)	the activity of using computers and other electronic equipment to store and send information
labour	/ˈleɪbə/	(n)	workers, especially people who do practical work with their hands
monopoly	/məˈnɒpəli/	(n)	when a company or organization is the only one in an area of business or activity and has complete control of it
multinational	/mʌltiˈnæʃənəl/	(adj)	active in several countries, or involving people from several countries
nowadays	/ˈnaʊədeɪz/	(adv)	at the present time, especially when compared to the past
obesity	/əʊˈbiːsəti/	(n)	the state of being extremely fat
outlet	/ˈaʊtlet/	(n)	a shop that is one of many owned by a particular company and that sells the goods which the company has produced
perfectionist	/pəˈfekʃənɪst/	(n)	someone who wants everything to be perfect
poverty	/ˈpɒvəti/	(n)	the condition of being extremely poor
prepared food	/prɪˈpeəd fuːd/	(n)	food made earlier
presently	/ˈprezəntli/	(adv)	now
refuse	/ˈrefjuːs/	(v)	to say that you will not do or accept something
remove	/rɪˈmuːv/	(v)	to take something away
selling point	/ˈselɪŋ pɔɪnt/	(n)	a characteristic of a product that will persuade people to buy it
separate	/ˈsepəreɪt/	(v)	to move apart, or to make people move apart
situated	/ˈsɪtjueɪtɪd/	(adj)	in a particular position
these days	/ðiːz deɪz/	(n)	used to talk about the present time
trade	/treɪd/	(n)	the activity of buying and selling, or exchanging, goods and/or services between people and countries

Vocabulary	Pronunciation	Part of speech	Definition
UNIT 2			
alternative	/ɔːlˈtɜːnətɪv/	(n)	one of two or more things that you can choose between
apprentice	/əˈprentɪs/	(n)	a person who is learning a job by working for someone who already has skills and experience
aspect	/ˈæspekt/	(n)	one part of a situation, problem, subject, etc.
assignment	/əˈsaɪnmənt/	(n)	a piece of work given to someone, especially as part of their studies or job
challenging	/ˈtʃælɪndʒɪŋ/	(adj)	difficult in a way that tests your ability or determination
component	/kəmˈpəʊnənt/	(n)	one of the parts or characteristics of something or someone
discussion	/dɪˈskʌʃən/	(n)	when people talk about something and tell each other their ideas or opinions
dissertation	/dɪsəˈteɪʃən/	(n)	a very long piece of writing done as part of a course of study
distinctive	/dɪˈstɪŋktɪv/	(n)	Something that is distinctive is easy to recognize because it is different from other things.
establishment	/ɪˈstæblɪʃmənt/	(n)	when an organization, school, business, etc. is started
examination	/ɪgzæmɪˈneɪʃən/	(n)	an exam
face-to-face	/feɪstəˈfeɪs/	(adj)	involving two people who are meeting in the same place
interaction	/ɪntərˈækʃən/	(n)	the activity of talking and doing things with other people, or the way you do this
journal	/ˈdʒɜːnəl/	(n)	a magazine containing articles about a particular subject
lecture	/ˈlektʃə/	(n)	a formal talk on a serious or specialist subject given to a group of people, especially students
lecturer	/ˈlektʃərə/	(n)	someone who teaches at a university or college
licence	/ˈlaɪsənts/	(n)	an official document that allows you to do or have something
module	/ˈmɒdjuːl/	(n)	a part of a university or college course
motivation	/məʊtɪˈveɪʃən/	(n)	the need or reason for doing something
permit	/ˈpɜːmɪt/	(n)	an official document that allows you to do something
plagiarism	/ˈpleɪdʒərɪzəm/	(n)	when someone copies someone else's work or ideas
principle	/ˈprɪntsəpəl/	(n)	a basic idea or rule that explains or controls how something happens or works
profession	/prəˈfeʃən/	(n)	a type of work that needs special training or education
scholarship	/ˈskɒləʃɪp/	(n)	an amount of money given to a person by an organization to pay for their education, usually at a college or university
semester	/sɪˈmestə/	(n)	one of the two time periods that a school or college year is divided into
seminar	/ˈsemɪnɑː/	(n)	a meeting of a group of people with a teacher or expert for training, discussion, or study of a subject
significant	/sɪgˈnɪfɪkənt/	(adj)	important or noticeable
specific	/spəˈsɪfɪk/	(adj)	used to refer to a particular thing and not something general
term	/tɜːm/	(n)	one of the periods of time that the school or university year is divided into
tuition fee	/tjuˈɪʃən fiː/	(n)	the money that you pay to be taught, especially in a college
tutor	/ˈtjuːtə/	(n)	someone who teaches one person or a very small group of people
tutorial	/tjuːˈtɔːriəl/	(n)	a class in which a small group of students talks about a subject with their tutor, especially at a British university
virtual	/ˈvɜːtjuəl/	(adj)	describes something that can be done or seen using a computer and therefore without going anywhere or talking to someone
vocational course	/vəʊˈkeɪʃənəl kɔːs/	(n)	a plan of study providing skills and education that prepare you for a job
UNIT 3			
adequate	/ˈædɪkwət/	(adj)	enough
complex	/ˈkɒmpleks/	(adj)	involving a lot of different but connected parts in a way that is difficult to understand
conventional	/kənˈventʃənəl/	(adj)	traditional and ordinary
cosmetic surgery	/kɒzˈmetɪk ˈsɜːdʒəri/	(n)	a medical operation to improve a person's appearance
disease	/dɪˈziːz/	(n)	(an) illness caused by infection or by a failure of health rather than by an accident
disease epidemic	/dɪˈziːz epɪˈdemɪk/	(n)	the appearance of a particular disease in a large number of people at the same time

Vocabulary	Pronunciation	Part of speech	Definition
illegal	/ɪˈliːgəl/	(adj)	not allowed by law
illness	/ˈɪlnəs/	(n)	a disease of the body or mind
medical	/ˈmedɪkəl/	(adj)	relating to medicine and different ways of curing illness
natural	/ˈnætʃərəl/	(adj)	Something that is natural exists or happens because of nature, not because it was made or done by people.
patent	/ˈpeɪtənt/	(n)	a legal right that a person or company receives to make or sell a particular product so that others cannot copy it
physical	/ˈfɪzɪkəl/	(adj)	related to the body
precise	/prɪˈsaɪs/	(adj)	exact and accurate
preventable illness	/prɪˈventəbəl ˈɪlnəs/	(n)	a disease of the body of mind which is able to be prevented
professional	/prəˈfeʃənəl/	(adj)	relating to a job that needs special training or education
remedy	/ˈremədi/	(n)	something that makes you better when you are ill
sedentary lifestyle	/ˈsedəntəri ˈlaɪfstaɪl/	(n)	someone's way of living involving little exercise or physical activity
synthetic	/sɪnˈθetɪk/	(adj)	not made from natural substances
treatment	/ˈtriːtmənt/	(n)	the use of drugs, exercises, etc. to cure a person of an illness or injury
underfunding	/ʌndəˈfʌndɪŋ/	(n)	a situation in which something is given less money than it needs
UNIT 4			
all-inclusive	/ɔːl ɪŋˈkluːsɪv/	(adj)	including everything
allow	/əˈlaʊ/	(v)	to give someone permission for something
authorize	/ˈɔːθəraɪz/	(v)	to give official permission for something
ban	/bæn/	(v)	to forbid something, especially officially
compulsory	/kəmˈpʌlsəri/	(adj)	If something is compulsory, you must do it because of a rule or law.
confusion	/kənˈfjuːʒən/	(n)	when people do not understand what is happening, what they should do or who someone or something is
contingency	/kənˈtɪndʒəntsi/	(n)	an event or situation that might happen in the future, especially one which could cause problems
criminalize	/ˈkrɪmɪnəlaɪz/	(v)	to make something illegal
cut it fine	/kʌt ɪt faɪn/	(ph)	to allow very little time for something
disorientating	/dɪˈsɔːriənteɪtɪŋ/	(adj)	making someone confused about where they are and where they are going
dissatisfaction	/dɪssætɪsˈfækʃən/	(n)	when someone is dissatisfied
exhilarating	/ɪgˈzɪləreɪtɪŋ/	(adj)	making you feel very excited and happy
grant	/grɑːnt/	(v)	to give or allow someone something, usually in an official way
great	/greɪt/	(adj)	large in amount, size or degree
harsh	/hɑːʃ/	(adj)	very cold, dangerous, or unpleasant and difficult to live in
infringe on	/ɪnˈfrɪndʒ ɒn/	(v)	If something infringes on someone's rights or freedom, it takes away some of their rights or limits their freedom.
legalize	/ˈliːgəlaɪz/	(v)	to make something legal
legislation	/ˌledʒɪˈsleɪʃən/	(n)	a law or set of laws suggested by a government and made official by a parliament
liable	/ˈlaɪəbəl/	(adj)	legally responsible
limit	/ˈlɪmɪt/	(v)	to control something so that it is less than a particular amount or number
objection	/əbˈdʒekʃən/	(n)	when someone says that they do not like or approve of something or someone
paragliding	/ˈpærəglaɪdɪŋ/	(n)	the sport of jumping out of an aircraft with a special parachute that allows you to travel a long horizontal distance before you land
permit	/pəˈmɪt/	(v)	to allow something
play (it) safe	/pleɪ seɪf/	(ph)	to be careful and not take risks
portfolio	/pɔːtˈfəʊliəʊ/	(n)	a collection of company shares and other investments that are owned by a particular person or organization
prevention	/prɪˈventʃən/	(n)	when you stop something from happening or stop someone from doing something
prohibit	/prəʊˈhɪbɪt/	(v)	to officially refuse to allow something
prudence	/ˈpruːdənts/	(n)	carefulness and avoidance risks

Vocabulary	Pronunciation	Part of speech	Definition
reduction	/rɪ'dʌkʃən/	(n)	when something is reduced
regulation	/regjə'leɪʃən/	(n)	an official rule that controls how something is done
responsibility	/rɪspɒntsə'bɪləti/	(n)	something that it is your job or duty to deal with
restrict	/rɪ'strɪkt/	(v)	to limit something
thrilling	/'θrɪlɪŋ/	(adj)	very exciting
uncomfortable	/ʌn'kʌmpftəbəl/	(adj)	not feeling comfortable and pleasant, or not making you feel comfortable and pleasant
uncontrolled	/ʌnkən'trəʊld/	(adj)	too strong or violent to be controlled

UNIT 5

Vocabulary	Pronunciation	Part of speech	Definition
alter	/'ɒltər/	(v)	to change, or to make someone or something change
consult	/kən'sʌlt/	(v)	to discuss something with someone before you make a decision
cultivate	/'kʌltɪveɪt/	(v)	to grow a particular crop
display	/dɪ'spleɪ/	(v)	to arrange something somewhere so that people can see it
distribute	/dɪ'strɪbjuːt/	(v)	to give something out to several people, or to spread or supply something
dry	/draɪ/	(v)	to make something become dry
emerge	/ɪ'mɜːdʒ/	(v)	to appear from somewhere or come out from somewhere
enhance	/ɪn'haːnts/	(v)	to improve something
extract	/ɪk'strækt/	(v)	to remove or take out something
ferment	/fə'ment/	(v)	If food or drink ferments, or if you ferment it, the sugar in it changes into alcohol because of a chemical process.
harvest	/'haːvɪst/	(v)	to pick and collect crops
grind	/graɪnd/	(v)	to make something into small pieces or a powder by pressing between hard surfaces
melt	/melt/	(v)	to turn from something solid into something soft or liquid
mould	/məʊld/	(v)	to make a soft substance a particular shape
package	/'pækɪdʒ/	(v)	to wrap an object in paper, usually in order to be sent by post
product	/'prɒdʌkt/	(n)	something that is made or grown to be sold
roast	/rəʊst/	(v)	If you roast food, you cook it in an oven or over a fire, and if food roasts, it is cooked in an oven or over a fire.
shell	/ʃel/	(v)	to remove peas, nuts, etc. from their shells or natural covering
temper	/'tempə/	(v)	to improve chocolate by heating it and cooling it again
undertake	/ʌndə'teɪk/	(v)	to do or begin to do something, especially something that will take a long time or be difficult

UNIT 6

Vocabulary	Pronunciation	Part of speech	Definition
ambitious	/æm'bɪʃəs/	(adj)	If a plan or idea is ambitious, it will need a lot of work and will be difficult to achieve.
community	/kə'mjuːnəti/	(n)	the people living in one particular area
control	/kən'trəʊl/	(v)	to order, limit or rule something, or someone's actions or behaviour
dam	/dæm/	(n)	a strong wall built across a river to stop the water and make a lake
disadvantage	/dɪsəd'vaːntɪdʒ/	(n)	something which makes a situation more difficult, or makes you less likely to succeed
disaster	/dɪ'zaːstə/	(n)	something that causes great harm or damage
disaster mitigation	/dɪ'zaːstə mɪtɪ'geɪʃən/	(n)	when people make an event that results in great harm or damage less harmful or bad
extraordinary	/ɪk'strɔːdənəri/	(adj)	very special, unusual or strange
extreme	/ɪk'striːm/	(adj)	the most unusual or the most serious possible
government report	/'gʌvənmənt rɪ'pɔːt/	(n)	a description of something or information about it given by the government
hurricane	/'hʌrɪkəɪn/	(n)	a violent storm with very strong winds
impossible	/ɪm'pɒsəbəl/	(adj)	If an action or event is impossible, it cannot happen or be done.
large-scale	/laːdʒ'skeɪl/	(adj)	involving a lot of people or happening in big numbers
levee	/'levi/	(n)	a wall made of land or other materials that is built next to a river to stop the river from flooding and covering everywhere in water

Vocabulary	Pronunciation	Part of speech	Definition
long-term	/lɒŋˈtɜːm/	(adj)	continuing a long time into the future
major	/ˈmeɪdʒə/	(adj)	more important, bigger or more serious than others of the same type
natural	/ˈnætʃərəl/	(adj)	Something that is natural exists or happens because of nature, not because it was made or done by people.
product manufacturing	/ˈprɒdʌkt mænjəˈfæktʃərɪŋ/	(n)	the business of producing goods in large numbers
prolong	/prəʊˈlɒŋ/	(v)	to make something last longer
relocation	/riːləʊˈkeɪʃən/	(n)	the act of moving to a new place
risk analysis	/rɪsk əˈnæləsɪs/	(n)	risk assessment
risk reduction	/rɪsk rɪˈdʌkʃən/	(n)	the act of making something less risky
sandbagging	/ˈsændbægɪŋ/	(n)	using bags filled with sand as a defence against floods
seasonal	/ˈsiːzənəl/	(adj)	relating to or happening during a particular period in the year
severe	/sɪˈvɪə/	(adj)	extremely bad
submerge	/səbˈmɜːdʒ/	(v)	to cause something to be under the surface of water, or to move below the surface of water
tsunami	/tsʊˈnɑːmi/	(n)	an extremely large wave from the sea which causes a lot of damage to buildings, etc. on land and is often caused by an earthquake
unpredictable	/ʌnprɪˈdɪktəbəl/	(adj)	changing so much that you do not know what will happen next

UNIT 7

Vocabulary	Pronunciation	Part of speech	Definition
affordable	/əˈfɔːdəbəl/	(adj)	cheap enough for most people to be able to buy
amenity	/əˈmiːnəti/	(n)	a building, piece of equipment, or service that is provided for people's comfort or enjoyment
architect	/ˈɑːkɪtekt/	(n)	someone whose job is to design buildings
architectural	/ɑːkɪˈtektʃərəl/	(adj)	relating to architecture
architecture	/ˈɑːkɪtektʃə/	(n)	the design and style of buildings
bathhouse	/ˈbɑːθhaʊs/	(n)	a public building where people can have a bath
compromise	/ˈkɒmprəmaɪz/	(v)	to allow your principles to be less strong or your standards or morals to be lower
conservation	/kɒntsəˈveɪʃən/	(n)	the protection of nature or ancient buildings
depress	/dɪˈpres/	(v)	to make someone feel very sad
depression	/dɪˈpreʃən/	(n)	when you feel very unhappy, or a mental illness that makes you feel very unhappy and anxious for long periods
durable	/ˈdʒʊərəbəl/	(adj)	remaining in good condition for a long time
efficiency	/ɪˈfɪʃəntsi/	(n)	when someone or something uses time and energy well, without wasting any
efficient	/ɪˈfɪʃənt/	(adj)	working or operating quickly and effectively in an organized way
emperor	/ˈempərə/	(n)	the male ruler of an empire
environment	/ɪnˈvaɪərənmənt/	(n)	the conditions that you live or work in and the way that they influence how you feel or how effectively you can work
the environment	/ðiː ɪnˈvaɪərənmənt/	(n)	the air, land and water where people, animals and plants live
environmental	/ɪnvaɪərənˈmentəl/	(adj)	relating to the environment
functionalism	/ˈfʌŋkʃənəlɪzəm/	(n)	the principle that the most important thing about an object such as a building is its use rather than what it looks like
green	/griːn/	(adj)	relating to nature and protecting the environment
green belt	/ˈgriːnbelt/	(n)	an area of land around a city or town where no new building is allowed
install	/ɪnˈstɔːl/	(v)	to put a piece of equipment somewhere and make it ready for use
marble	/ˈmɑːbəl/	(n)	hard, smooth stone which is often used for decoration
mosque	/mɒsk/	(n)	a building for Islamic religious activities and worship
mud	/mʌd/	(n)	a thick liquid mixture of soil and water, or this mixture after it has dried
outskirts	/ˈaʊtskɜːts/	(n)	the outer area of a city or town
palace	/ˈpælɪs/	(n)	a very large building where a king, queen or president lives
responsible	/rɪˈspɒntsəbəl/	(adj)	showing good judgment and able to be trusted
responsibly	/rɪˈspɒntsəbli/	(adv)	in a way that shows you have good judgment and can be trusted
skyscraper	/ˈskaɪskreɪpə/	(n)	a very tall building

Vocabulary	Pronunciation	Part of speech	Definition
solar panel	/ˈsəʊlə ˈpænəl/	(n)	a piece of equipment that changes light from the sun into electricity
straw	/strɔː/	(n)	the long, dried stems of plants such as wheat, often given to animals for sleeping on and eating
structural engineer	/ˈstrʌktʃərəl endʒɪˈnɪə/	(n)	a person who is specially trained to examine buildings and discover if there are any problems with their structure
sultan	/ˈsʌltən/	(n)	a ruler in some Muslim countries
tile	/taɪl/	(n)	one of the flat, square pieces that are used for covering roofs, floors, or walls
tomb	/tuːm/	(n)	a place where a dead person is buried, usually with a stone structure
tower	/ˈtaʊə/	(n)	a very tall, narrow building, or part of a building
urban sprawl	/ˈɜːbən sprɔːl/	(n)	the careless or untidy spread of a town or city

UNIT 8

alternative	/ɔːlˈtɜːnətɪv/	(adj)	different from what is usual or traditional
biofuel	/ˈbaɪəʊfjuːəl/	(n)	fuel produced from plant material
canola oil	/kəˈnəʊlə ɔɪl/	(n)	a type of oil made from a variety of rapeseed that can be used for cooking or as a biofuel
carbon footprint	/ˈkɑːbən ˈfʊtprɪnt/	(n)	the amount of energy that a person or organization uses in order to exist or operate
carbon neutral	/ˈkɑːbən ˈnjuːtrəl/	(adj)	not producing carbon emissions
consult	/kənˈsʌlt/	(v)	to get information or advice from a person, book, etc. with special knowledge on a particular subject
consumption	/kənˈsʌmpʃən/	(n)	the amount of something that someone uses, eats, or drinks
contest	/kənˈtest/	(v)	If you contest a formal statement, a claim, a judge's decision, or a legal case, you say formally that it is wrong or unfair and try to have it changed.
cooperative	/kəʊˈɒpərətɪv/	(n)	a company that is owned and managed by the people who work in it
diesel	/ˈdiːzəl/	(n)	fuel used in the engines of some vehicles, especially buses and lorries
energy	/ˈenədʒi/	(n)	the power that comes from electricity, gas, etc.
fuel	/ˈfjuːəl/	(n)	a substance that is burned to provide heat or power
hydroelectricity	/haɪdrəʊɪlekˈtrɪsɪti/	(n)	electricity produced by the force of fast moving water such as rivers or waterfalls
petrol	/ˈpetrəl/	(n)	a liquid fuel used in cars
pollution	/pəˈluːʃən/	(n)	damage caused to water, air, etc. by harmful substances or waste
production	/prəˈdʌkʃən/	(n)	when you make or grow something
solar power	/ˈsəʊlə ˈpaʊə/	(n)	solar energy
source	/sɔːs/	(n)	where something comes from
wind turbine	/wɪnd ˈtɜːbaɪn/	(n)	a machine with long parts at the top that are turned by the wind, used to make electricity

UNIT 9

abstract	/ˈæbstrækt/	(adj)	Abstract art involves shapes and colours and not images of real things or people.
aesthetic	/iːsˈθetɪk/	(adj)	relating to beauty and the way something looks
avant-garde	/ˌævãːŋˈgɑːd/	(adj)	If art, music, etc. is avant-garde, it is new and unusual in style.
banal	/bəˈnɑːl/	(adj)	ordinary and not exciting
calligraphy	/kəˈlɪgrəfi/	(n)	(the art of producing) beautiful writing, often created with a special pen or brush
cart	/kɑːt/	(n)	a wooden or metal structure on wheels that is used for carrying things
claim	/kleɪm/	(v)	to say that something is true or is a fact, although you cannot prove it and other people might not believe it
creative	/kriˈeɪtɪv/	(adj)	producing or using original and unusual ideas
decorative	/ˈdekərətɪv/	(adj)	made to look attractive
describe	/dɪˈskraɪb/	(v)	to say or write what someone or something is like
discuss	/dɪˈskʌs/	(v)	to talk about something with someone and tell each other your ideas or opinions

Vocabulary	Pronunciation	Part of speech	Definition
established	/ɪˈstæblɪʃt/	(adj)	accepted or respected because of having existed for a long period of time
figurative	/ˈfɪɡjərətɪv/	(adj)	Figurative art shows people, places, or things in a similar way to how they look in real life.
genius	/ˈdʒiːniəs/	(n)	someone who is extremely intelligent or extremely good at doing something
illustrate	/ˈɪləstreɪt/	(v)	to draw pictures for a book, magazine, etc. or to put pictures, photographs, etc. in a book, magazine, etc.
laser	/ˈleɪzə/	(n)	a machine that produces a strong beam of light that has medical and technical uses or a beam of light produced by a machine like this
lifelike	/ˈlaɪflaɪk/	(adj)	If something is lifelike, it looks real.
mechanical	/mɪˈkænɪkəl/	(adj)	relating to or operated by machines
mechanism	/ˈmekənɪzəm/	(n)	a part of a piece of equipment that does a particular job
monumental	/mɒnjəˈmentəl/	(adj)	very large
moving	/ˈmuːvɪŋ/	(adj)	causing strong feelings of sadness or sympathy
objective	/əbˈdʒektɪv/	(adj)	only influenced by facts and not by feelings
poetry	/ˈpəʊətri/	(n)	poems in general as a form of literature
pottery	/ˈpɒtəri/	(n)	plates, bowls, etc. that are made from clay, or the activity or skill of making things out of clay
prove	/pruːv/	(v)	to show that something is true
sculptor	/ˈskʌlptə/	(n)	someone who makes sculpture
sculpture	/ˈskʌlptʃə/	(n)	a piece of art that is made from stone, wood, clay, etc. or the process of making objects like this
self-propelled	/self prəˈpeld/	(adj)	able to move by its own power
shortcut	/ˈʃɔːtkʌt/	(n)	a quicker way of getting somewhere or doing something
specific	/spəˈsɪfɪk/	(adj)	used to refer to a particular thing and not something general
split	/splɪt/	(v)	to divide into smaller parts or groups, or to divide something into smaller parts or groups
spring	/sprɪŋ/	(n)	a piece of curved or bent metal that can be pressed into a smaller space but then returns to its usual shape
time-consuming	/ˈtaɪmkənsjuːmɪŋ/	(adj)	needing a lot of time
weaving	/ˈwiːvɪŋ/	(n)	the activity of making cloth by repeatedly crossing a single thread through two sets of long threads on a loom

UNIT 10

Vocabulary	Pronunciation	Part of speech	Definition
decline	/dɪˈklaɪn/	(v)	to gradually become less or worse
demographic	/deməʊˈɡræfɪk/	(n)	a group of people, for example customers, who are similar in age, social class, etc.
demographic	/ˌdeməˈɡræfɪk/	(adj)	used to refer to changes in the number of births, marriages, deaths, etc. in a particular area during a period of time
economic impact	/iːkəˈnɒmɪk ɪmˈpækt/	(n)	A financial effect that something, especially something new, has on a situation or person.
elderly	/ˈeldəli/	(adj)	a more polite word for 'old', used to describe people
the elderly	/ðiː ˈeldəli/	(ph)	people who are elderly
focus on	/ˈfəʊkəs ɒn/	(v)	to give a lot of attention to one particular person, subject or thing
healthcare	/ˈhelθkeə/	(n)	the set of services provided by a country or an organization for treating people who are ill
identify with	/aɪˈdentɪfaɪ wɪð/	(v)	to feel that you are similar to someone in some way and that you can understand them or their situation because of this
in brief	/ɪn briːf/	(ph)	using only a few words
in contrast	/ɪn ˈkɒntrɑːst/	(ph)	showing an obvious difference between two or more things
in theory	/ɪn ˈθɪəri/	(ph)	If something is possible in theory, it should be possible, but often it does not happen in that way.
pension	/ˈpentʃən/	(n)	a sum of money paid regularly by the government or a private company to a person who has stopped working because they are old or ill
protect	/prəˈtekt/	(v)	to keep someone or something safe from something dangerous or bad
range	/reɪndʒ/	(n)	a group of different things of the same general type

Vocabulary	Pronunciation	Part of speech	Definition
rely on	/rɪˈlaɪ ɒn/	(v)	to need a particular thing or the help and support of someone or something in order to continue, to work correctly, or succeed
retirement	/rɪˈtaɪəmənt/	(n)	when you leave your job and stop working, usually because you are old
shortage	/ˈʃɔːtɪdʒ/	(n)	when there is not enough of something
social activities	/ˈsəʊʃəl ækˈtɪvətiz/	(n)	leisure activities that people do with others
sum up	/sʌm ʌp/	(v)	to describe briefly the important facts or characteristics of something or someone
unemployment	/ʌnɪmˈplɔɪmənt/	(n)	the number of people who are unemployed, or the state of being unemployed
workforce	/ˈwɜːkfɔːs/	(n)	all the people who work in a company, organization or country

UNIT 1 A WORLD OF FOOD IN ONE CITY

Narrator: New York: from melting pot to cooking pot. As international trade routes, migration, media and IT communication expand across traditional borders, different cultures interact more, with a flow of goods, labour and ideas. This is called globalization.

Although this is common all over the world, there are certain cities where this is more obvious than others. New York is perhaps the best example of a city where different cultures have come together through globalization. A centre for migration for many centuries, New York is home to many ethnic groups often living in the same neighbourhoods.

This can be clearly seen by the huge variety of world food on sale. Immigrants from Central Europe, South America, Italy, the Caribbean and China have brought their food with them. New York often took these recipes and gave them a twist to create a new American identity such as ice cream sundaes, burgers and hot dogs.

There are over 19 thousand restaurants in New York and every type of international food is represented: South American, Irish, Middle Eastern and Indian. In Harlem there are famous restaurants serving Afro-American food with chicken and rice dishes. Some have even developed into brands selling prepared food in supermarkets and recipe books.

New York has always been called a 'melting pot' as different communities have come together in one city. This means that all different ingredients, recipe books and cooking equipment are available in the shops and markets.

UNIT 2 BECOMING A GONDOLIER

Narrator: Gondolas are a traditional form of transport along the canals of Venice in Italy. The people who steer the boats are called gondoliers. They play an important role in Venetian life and so they have a high status in the city. Being a gondolier is a prestigious and well paid job. Gondolas are privately owned and the profession usually passes from father to son. There are just 425 members of the profession in the whole city, and it is very rare for a woman to be a gondolier.

Becoming a gondolier takes years of practice because it is a very skilled job. Apprentice gondoliers have to take an exam before they can join the profession. Passing the exam is incredibly difficult and only three people pass each year. Alessandro has been an apprentice for three years. Unusually, he is the first in his family to train to be a gondolier. He has had an experienced gondolier teaching him.

Alessandro: It's my dream to be a gondolier. It will make me very proud.

Narrator: It is the day of the exam. Alessandro is nervous. If he passes the exam, his family will be able to stay in Venice. If he fails, they will have to move out of Venice and find work elsewhere. The examiners watch his skills carefully. He must show how well he can steer the boat. The canals are very narrow, and Alessandro must be careful not to touch the sides, or he will lose marks. Other obstacles are low bridges and building work. It is the moment of truth, and Alessandro will find out if he has passed his exam or not.

Examiner: We've discussed your exam result, and we're pleased to let you know that you're a gondolier! Well done!

Narrator: The three years of hard training have paid off. Alessandro is now a fully qualified gondolier, and proudly wears the distinctive uniform of stripy shirt and straw hat. He can now provide for his family and settle down in Venice, his home town.

UNIT 3 ALTERNATIVE MEDICINE

Narrator: Ayurveda, from India, is the oldest form of medicine on the planet. Its name means roughly 'the science of long life'. It is over 3,500 years old and people still use it today. Now, in India, there are over 300,000 trained Ayurveda doctors and the practice has spread to alternative health centres around the world. Most of its remedies are from plants, herbs and other natural ingredients. Using plants to treat and heal diseases is not only something that Ayurveda doctors do.

People around the world use natural products in medicine. This shaman in the Peruvian rainforest also uses the things that grow around him to treat patients, using a wide range of medicines. Here in the Serengeti in Africa, we can see how people use natural resources for the same reasons.

In fact, a huge number of treatments used in what we might call 'modern medicine' come from plants – often these are the remedies used by our ancestors. For example, aspirin, one of the most common painkillers, is based on plant extracts from the bark of willow trees. Hundreds of common medicines are plant-based.

While we can learn a lot from these ancient forms of medicine, we should always be careful. The cures have not always been tested scientifically so there is a risk that using one of these ancient remedies could have no effect – or worse, could actually be dangerous. Scientists worry that some natural medicines may contain heavy metals such as lead and mercury.

Nevertheless, nature is clearly a valuable source of medicine, bringing benefits to people all over the world.

UNIT 4 ROLLER COASTERS

Narrator: Why do we find it fun to scare ourselves on roller coasters?

All over the world people love roller coasters. The twists, turns, ups and downs at speed are all disorientating and at times uncomfortable. Yet when we get off the ride we feel great and cannot wait to get on again.

Throughout history, human beings have often found themselves at risk being hunted by wild animals such as wolves, victims of natural disasters or subjected to harsh weather.

In extreme circumstances with stress, fear or pain, the body produces natural chemicals. The hormone adrenalin helps the body perform better, meaning people are more alert and able to run faster or are stronger. Additionally, the body's natural painkillers, endorphins, are produced. These not only help the body withstand pain and discomfort but also make people feel good.

Roller coasters trick the body into feeling fear, and so into producing endorphins. This enables people to experience exhilaration without putting themselves in serious danger. There are strict controls on the design and forces which can be used on roller coasters during the planning stage and meticulous safety checks and inspections are carried out daily once the ride is built.

In the modern world we have developed ways to experience danger and push our bodies to the limits to generate the feeling of exhilaration. This might be cave diving at a depth of 400 feet, sledging in the snow, driving fast cars, running with bulls, or aerobatics in small planes.

Roller coasters, however, are perhaps the most accessible form of thrills. The advantage of roller coasters is that they change the way the body feels with rapid results and they offer thrills without risk.

UNIT 5 MAKING CHOCOLATE

Narrator: Chocolate production begins with the harvesting of cocoa pods from trees. It is grown in rain forests in countries on the equator such as Ghana, Ivory Coast, Brazil and Indonesia. The pods contain beans which are fermented and dried in the sun for a week or more. At this stage, the beans taste bitter and nothing like chocolate. Once dried, the beans are transported in large sacks and sold to chocolate producers all over the world.

In the chocolate factory, before production begins, a sample of beans is tested by splitting them so the inside is revealed. In a good bean, the insides are clearly separated. This shows that the fermentation has worked and has begun to remove the bean's natural bitterness. The beans are washed, then roasted. Roasting is the most important part of the process. It is critical that the beans are roasted at the correct temperature otherwise the taste is adversely affected.

As the beans are roasted, the amino acids and sugars found in the beans begin to react together to form the familiar chocolate flavour. The roasted beans are then shelled and the centre or 'nib' is what is left. The nibs need to go through a grinder to make them into a liquid.

At this stage, extra cocoa butter is added to help make the final chocolate texture as smooth as possible. The next stage is when the chocolate liquid, milk and sugar, which are required to make chocolate, are mixed together.

The resulting chocolate paste is then passed through rollers and turned into a powder.

The chocolate powder is mixed with milk powder and heated. This is called conching and can last up to a week. The acidity helps turn the mixture into a liquid chocolate syrup. This is then tempered. Tempering is when the chocolate is heated, cooled and gradually heated again to a warm temperature. Tempering is the secret of quality chocolate.

The change of temperature enables the fats to crystallize which results in large bars of chocolate. Industrial chocolate producers will then sell these slabs to chocolate specialists.

The chocolate bars are melted again by tempering and then can be moulded to make individual chocolates. At this stage, fillings can be added in between layers of chocolate. Finally, when the chocolates are finished, they are left to set in trays ready to be packaged, sold and eaten.

UNIT 6 THE THREE GORGES DAM

Narrator: The Yangtze river in China is the world's third longest river. It is beautiful, with a rich history. As a major trade route, it provides jobs for many people who live along it. However, the river is unpredictable and in the past has often flooded, resulting in the death and homelessness of many local people. In 1998, there was a particularly bad flood when 300 million people were displaced.

The Chinese government had already decided to control the floods by building a dam. Construction of the Three Gorges dam began in 1994. Completed in 2008, the dam controls the flow of water in the Yangtze and protects the inhabitants in the area below it from flooding.

One additional advantage is that it now provides cheap, clean electricity through the world's biggest hydroelectric power station built into the dam. It provides 10% of China's electricity.

One of the disadvantages is that in order to achieve the building of the dam, much of the surrounding area behind the dam needed to be submerged. This meant the loss of 13 cities and numerous towns and villages with the relocation of 2 million people. Thousands of years of cultural heritage in the form of ancient buildings were also lost.

This extraordinary engineering project is an example of what can be achieved with sufficient planning and vision. The dam has resulted in increased security for inhabitants living along the river and provided an additional source of much needed energy, but this has not been without a cost.

UNIT 7 ISLAMIC ARCHITECTURE

Narrator: Islamic architecture has been built in a wide range of styles from the foundation of Islam to the present day. The main Islamic architectural types are: the palace, the mosque and the tomb.

One of the greatest Islamic palaces is the Alhambra in Spain. *Alhambra* means 'the red one' in Arabic. It was built during the fourteenth century by the rulers of the Emirate of Granada. These days it is a popular tourist destination.

The buildings were designed to reflect the beauty of paradise. The extensive gardens, for which a special irrigation system was built, contain many fountains and pools. And water channels inside the buildings themselves acted as air conditioning, helping to keep the rooms in the Alhambra cool.

The magnificent decoration consists of leaves and trees, Arabic writing and beautiful delicate patterns. And yet from the outside, the building simply looks like a fortress, with 13 huge impressive towers.

Islamic architecture is also famous for religious buildings. The Sultan Ahmed Mosque is a historical mosque in Istanbul, the largest city in Turkey. The mosque is known as the Blue Mosque for the blue tiles which cover the inside walls. It was built between 1609 and 1616, during the rule of Ahmed I. The writing on the walls is originally by the great seventeenth-century calligrapher Ametli Kasım Gubarım.

A heavy iron chain hangs in the entrance on the western side. The chain was put there so that the sultan, who rode in on a horse, had to lower his head to enter the mosque.

Perhaps the finest example of Islamic tomb architecture is the Taj Mahal in India. It was built by Mughal emperor Shah Jahan in memory of his wife. The building is covered with designs in paint, carved marble and precious stones.

It was constructed using materials from India, China, Afghanistan and the gulf of Arabia. The architects came from Turkey, Iran and Pakistan and it was built by 10,000 Indian workers. The Taj Mahal perfectly demonstrates how the ideas of Islamic architecture spread around the world.

UNIT 8 ALTERNATIVE ENERGY

Narrator: As the world's population increases, so too does the demand for energy. Traditionally, energy resources have been non-renewable fossil fuels such as oil, coal and gas. As they begin to run out, the search for cleaner, renewable energy resources becomes more urgent.

Solar energy and biofuels are just two of many alternative energies that could help solve the world's energy crisis. As with traditional fossil fuels, large solar power plants can be built to supply energy directly to a country's national electricity network.

But solar power can also work on a much smaller scale. In Mount Pleasant, Washington, the whole neighbourhood formed a cooperative, a volunteer community organization, so that everyone could benefit from solar energy. Many of the residents had solar panels installed on their roofs. As a result they benefit from free electricity at source, and they can sell any electricity they don't use back to the power company. This resident has saved 80% on his electricity bill!

Transport and travel are a huge drain on the world's energy resources, so it is important to find an alternative, renewable energy source for cars. Biofuel can be used as a replacement for petrol and diesel and is being produced using canola flowers. These flowers can be grown close to the end user so transport costs are low, and energy wastage limited. They are also carbon neutral: the amount of carbon they produce when burnt is equal to the amount they absorb when growing.

With most countries still very reliant on old forms of energy, both individuals and governments face a huge challenge. But the developments in solar and biofuel energies give us hope for a cleaner future.

UNIT 9 A LEONARDO DA VINCI DESIGN

Narrator: Leonardo da Vinci was a genius. He is famous today as a great painter but he was also a sculptor, architect, musician, mathematician, engineer, writer, scientist and inventor. His inventions were hundreds of years ahead of their time but many were never made.

This team of engineers is going to put a Leonardo da Vinci design to the test using the materials which were available 500 years ago.

The engineers are shown da Vinci's design of a self-propelled cart. They immediately see a problem. It looks like da Vinci didn't decide whether to have three or five wheels. The team decides to split into two to test both designs. They suggest a race to find the winner.

First, they use a computer to turn da Vinci's design into modern engineering plans and then start to make the wheels for the cart.

Making the wheels is more difficult than the teams thought.

Making the drive mechanism looks even more difficult but while one team cuts the wood

with a time-consuming traditional method, the other team has a shortcut in mind.

They use the laser cutter to save time making the cogs in the mechanism. The metal springs provide the power for the mechanism but one team is nervous when they wind their powerful spring as it could break the cart or cause an injury.

The other team manages to get both springs working and their cart is finished.

On the evening of the race, both teams wind the springs in their carts. However one team loses count and winds the spring up too much, breaking it. They decide to run the race on one spring anyway.

The result is in no doubt. While one team's cart starts quicker, their lack of power means that the other team's cart wins the race comfortably. The teams prove the genius of Leonardo da Vinci's 500-year-old design.

UNIT 10 THE KHANTY OF SIBERIA

Narrator: The Russian Federation is by far the biggest country in the world. It is twice the size of the United States of America and contains 11 time zones.

Siberia is a vast region in the centre and east of the Russian Federation. It is famous for its freezing winters. Temperatures can drop as low as −60 °C. In the Ugra, in the centre of west Siberia, where temperatures are below freezing for up to seven months of the year, live the Khanty people.

The Khanty live as their ancestors lived. A way of life that hasn't changed for centuries. There are 28,000 Khanty people living today. Alexei and Dulcia Moldanov are among them. They have 200 reindeer. In the coldest months of the year, they keep them in the forest. In the summer, the reindeer and the Moldanovs wander together. The Moldanovs live here in the winter, without gas, electricity or telephones. But they enjoy being outside with their reindeer. But they are getting older and they need help. Their son Misha lives with his family, in a small village, two hundred miles away. The village has only one road and one shop.

Misha and his son Daniil are going to visit Misha's parents. The trip gives Misha the opportunity to teach his six-year-old son about Alexei and Dulcia's traditional way of life. It is a long journey from the village to the forest. Misha and Daniil travel by snowmobile across the snow and ice of Siberia.

There is work for Misha to do. He must repair the reindeer pen in order to stop the animals from escaping. He also helps with rounding the animals up, which is something that Alexei cannot do alone. When Daniil has grown up, Misha will go to live in the forest. Will Daniil one day choose the same life?

The future is uncertain. The Khanty way of life is threatened by the modern world. But the more Daniil sees of the forest, the more he will be inspired to protect it.

ACKNOWLEDGEMENTS

Author acknowledgements

For their love, support (and occasionally early bedtimes), I would like to thank Fitz, Olivia and Amy. Thanks also to Lipton Zee. From Cambridge University Press, I am grateful to Barry Tadman, Fran Disken, Frances Amrani, Ruth Cox and Janet Weller for their skill and expertise in helping to shape the final text.
Chris Sowton

Publisher's acknowledgements

The publishers are extremely grateful to the following people and their students for reviewing and trialling this course during its development. The course has benefited hugely from your insightful comments, advice and feedback.

Mr M.K. Adjibade, King Saud University, Saudi Arabia; Canan Aktug, Bursa Technical University, Turkey; Olwyn Alexander, Heriot Watt University, UK; Valerie Anisy, Damman University, Saudi Arabia; Anwar Al-Fetlawi, University of Sharjah, UAE; Laila Al-Qadhi, Kuwait University, Kuwait; Tahani Al-Taha, University of Dubai, UAE; Ozlem Atalay, Middle East Technical University, Turkey; Seda Merter Ataygul, Bursa Technical University Turkey; Harika Altug, Bogazici University, Turkey; Kwab Asare, University of Westminster, UK; Erdogan Bada, Cukurova University, Turkey; Cem Balcikanli, Gazi University, Turkey; Gaye Bayri, Anadolu University, Turkey; Meher Ben Lakhdar, Sohar University, Oman; Emma Biss, Girne American University, UK; Dogan Bulut, Meliksah University, Turkey; Sinem Bur, TED University, Turkey; Alison Chisholm, University of Sussex, UK; Dr. Panidnad Chulerk , Rangsit University, Thailand; Sedat Cilingir, Bilgi University, Istanbul, Turkey; Sarah Clark, Nottingham Trent International College, UK; Elaine Cockerham, Higher College of Technology, Muscat, Oman; Asli Derin, Bilgi University, Turkey; Steven Douglass, University of Sunderland, UK; Jacqueline Einer, Sabanci University, Turkey; Basak Erel, Anadolu University, Turkey; Hande Lena Erol, Piri Reis Maritime University, Turkey; Gulseren Eyuboglu, Ozyegin University, Turkey; Muge Gencer, Kemerburgaz University, Turkey; Jeff Gibbons, King Fahed University of Petroleum and Minerals, Saudi Arabia; Maxine Gilway, Bristol University, UK; Dr Christina Gitsaki, HCT, Dubai Men's College, UAE; Sam Fenwick, Sohar University, Oman; Peter Frey, International House, Doha, Qatar; Neil Harris, Swansea University, UK; Vicki Hayden, College of the North Atlantic, Qatar; Joud Jabri-Pickett, United Arab Emirates University, Al Ain, UAE; Aysel Kilic, Anadolu University, Turkey; Ali Kimav, Anadolu University, Turkey; Bahar Kiziltunali, Izmir University of Economics, Turkey; Kamil Koc, Ozel Kasimoglu Coskun Lisesi, Turkey; Ipek Korman-Tezcan, Yeditepe University, Turkey; Philip Lodge, Dubai Men's College, UAE; Iain Mackie, Al Rowdah University, Abu Dhabi, UAE; Katherine Mansfield, University of Westminster, UK; Kassim Mastan, King Saud University, Saudi Arabia; Elspeth McConnell, Newham College, UK; Lauriel Mehdi, American University of Sharjah, UAE; Dorando Mirkin-Dick, Bell International Institute, UK; Dr Sita Musigrungsi, Prince of Songkla University, Hatyai, Thailand; Mark Neville, Al Hosn University, Abu Dhabi, UAE; Shirley Norton, London School of English, UK; James Openshaw, British Study Centres, UK; Hale Ottolini, Mugla Sitki Kocman University, Turkey; David Palmer, University of Dubai, UAE; Michael Pazinas, United Arab Emirates University, UAE; Troy Priest, Zayed University, UAE; Alison Ramage Patterson, Jeddah, Saudi Arabia; Paul Rogers, Qatar Skills Academy, Qatar; Josh Round, Saint George International, UK; Harika Saglicak, Bogazici University, Turkey; Asli Saracoglu, Isik University, Turkey; Neil Sarkar, Ealing, Hammersmith and West London College, UK; Nancy Shepherd, Bahrain University, Bahrain; Jonathan Smith, Sabanci University, Turkey; Peter Smith, United Arab Emirates University, UAE; Adem Soruc, Fatih University Istanbul, Turkey; Dr Peter Stanfield, HCT, Madinat Zayed & Ruwais Colleges, UAE; Maria Agata Szczerbik, United Arab Emirates University, Al Ain, UAE; Burcu Tezcan-Unal, Bilgi University, Turkey; Dr Nakonthep Tipayasuparat, Rangsit University, Thailand; Scott Thornbury, The New School, New York, USA; Susan Toth, HCT, Dubai Men's Campus, Dubai, UAE; Melin Unal, Ege University, Izmir, Turkey; Aylin Unaldi, Bogaziçi University, Turkey; Colleen Wackrow, Princess Nourah bint Abdulrahman University, Riyadh, Saudi Arabia; Gordon Watts, Study Group, Brighton UK; Po Leng Wendelkin, INTO at University of East Anglia, UK; Halime Yildiz, Bilkent University, Ankara, Turkey; Ferhat Yilmaz, Kahramanmaras Sutcu Imam University, Turkey.

Special thanks to Peter Lucantoni for sharing his expertise, both pedagogical and cultural.

Text and Photo acknowledgements

The authors and publishers acknowledge the following sources of copyright material and are grateful for the permissions granted. While every effort has been made, it has not always been possible to identify the sources of all the material used, or to trace all copyright holders. If any omissions are brought to our notice, we will be happy to include the appropriate acknowledgements on reprinting.

p.12: (1) © Eric Limon/Shutterstock; p.12: (2) © szefai/Shutterstock; p.12: (3) © Steven Vidler/Eurasia Press/Corbis. pp.14/15: © Yamanda Taro/Getty; p.19(L): © Joel Carillet/Getty; p.19(R): © Jake Curtis/Getty; p.21: © Gevenme/Getty; pp.32/33: © Maximillian Stock Ltd/Science Faction/Corbis; p.40(B): © Peter Muller/Getty; p.40(T): © Hill Street Studios/Getty; pp.50/51: © Lee Frost/Robert Harding World Imagery/ Corbis; p.54(TL): © Temmuz Can Arsiray/Getty; p.54(TR): Creative Studio/Getty; p.58: © Rick Gomez/Corbis; pp.68/69: © Buzz Pictures/ Alamy; p.73(T): © John Lamm/Transtock/Corbis; p.73(B): © John & Tina Reid/Getty; p.73(CR): © Jack Hollingsworth/Corbis; p.76(R): © Adrian Myers/Getty; p.76(L): © Win-Initiative/Getty; p.86/87: © Louie Psihoyos/Corbis; p.90: © Jose Fuste Raga/Corbis; p.91: © Suzan Oschmann/Shutterstock; p.94: © Sue Bennett/Alamy; pp.104/105: Education Images/Getty; p.108(1): Thinkstock; p.108(2): © Michael Runkel/Imagebroker/Corbis; p.108(3): Skyscan/Corbis; p.108(4): © Mainichi Newspaper/Corbis; p.108(5): © Raziomov/Shutterstock; p.108(6): © Jens Buttner/Corbis; pp.122/123: © Maremagnum/ Getty; p.128(BL): © Howard Harrison/Alamy; p.128(TR): © Jose L Pelaez/Corbis; p.131(T): © Barry Winniker/Getty; p.131(B): © Alan Weintraub/Arcaid/Corbis; pp.140/141: Bettmann/Corbis; p.144: © Ed Darack/Science Faction/Corbis; p.148(T): © Stockbyte/Getty; p.148(C): © AFP/Getty; p.148(B): © F1Digitale Bildagentur GmbH/Alamy; pp.158/159: © Tim E White/Getty; p.162(TL): © Burstein Collection/ Corbis; p.162(TR): © Andy Rain/epa/Corbis; p.162(BL): © Elliott Erwitt/Magnum Photos; p.162(BR): © Alex Segre/Alamy; p.163: © Bruno Ehrs/Corbis; p.166: © Henri Cartier-Bresson/Magnum Photos; p.171: Popperfoto/Getty; p.172: © Dennis Hallinan/Alamy; pp.176/177: © Pierre Jacques/Hemis/Corbis; p.181(BL): © Afton Alamaraz/ Getty; p.181(TR): © Asia Images Group plc Ltd/Alamy; p.181(BR): © Thepalmer/Getty; p.193: © Celia Paterson/Arabian Eye/Corbis.

All videos stills by kind permission of © Discovery Communications LLC 2013

Illustrations

Rick Capanni (HL Studios) pp.163, 169, 170, 173, 187, 190, 191; Oxford Designers & Illustrators pp.24, 28; Simon Tegg pp.78, 82, 89

Corpus

Development of this publication has made use of the Cambridge English Corpus (CEC). The CEC is a multi-billion word computer database of contemporary spoken and written English. It includes British English, American English and other varieties of English. It also includes the Cambridge Learner Corpus, developed in collaboration with Cambridge English Language Assessment. Cambridge University Press has built up the CEC to provide evidence about language use that helps to produce better language teaching materials.

Dictionary

Cambridge dictionaries are the world's most widely used dictionaries for learners of English. Available at three levels (Cambridge Essential English Dictionary, Cambridge Learner's Dictionary and Cambridge Advanced Learner's Dictionary), they provide easy-to-understand definitions, example sentences, and help in avoiding typical mistakes. The dictionaries are also available online at dictionary.cambridge.org. © Cambridge University Press, reproduced with permission.

Photo research by Alison Prior

Typeset by emc design ltd